DREAMS ON FIRE
EMBERS OF HOPE

DREAMS ON FIRE
EMBERS OF HOPE

From the Pulpits of Los Angeles After the Riots

Edited by Ignacio Castuera

Chalice Press
St. Louis, Missouri

Cover design: Michael A. Dominguez
Cover photo: © 1992 Marissa Roth

Printed in the United States of America

Acknowledgments

It took a titanic effort to gather all these materials, transcribe them, load them into a computer, mail them, etc. within little more than a week. It took a team effort, one that demonstrates clearly that people of different ethnic and religious backgrounds can work together for a common goal that benefits all.

Many people were part of that team, but the following deserve special acknowledgment: Frances Bass, who transcribed most of the material. Daniel Trent, who also helped in transcribing and loading into the computer. Grace Baldwin and Kym Sawtelle, who ran necessary errands. Jean Lamb and Ruth Shaw, who covered the office at the church and kept it going while I was absorbed in getting the sermons compiled and collected. Bill Feitz, who provided the necessary incantations to make the computers work when they did not seem to want to, and who graciously made his FAX machine available. Attorney Robert Sills, who also provided suggestions for photographers and allowed me to use his FAX machine. A special thank you goes to the staff of the Southern California Inter-Faith Task Force on Central America: Freddie Schrider and Mary Brent Wehrli provided referrals and paved the way when necessary.

Finally, a very special thank you to David Polk, whose guidance and encouragement were the most valuable asset I could have possibly had. It is indeed providential that a seminary friendship culminates in a collaboration as timely and exciting as this one was.

Ignacio Castuera
Hollywood, California
May 17, 1992

Contents

Foreword

Harvey Cox

> *"God gave Noah the rainbow sign.*
> *No more water,*
> *The fire next time."*
>   *African-American spiritual*

What does the fire mean? For people whose lives are shaped by the biblical narratives, the fire can mean many different things. Flame signifies destruction and judgment, the kind that fell upon the cities of Sodom and Gomorrah. It can also mean purification or—as in the case of Shadrach, Meshach, and Abednego—an occasion for the testing of faith. It can mean divine guidance, like the pillar of fire that led the Hebrews through the wilderness at night. Tongues of flame can become bearers of the Holy Spirit descending with power, as it did on the occasion of Pentecost in the Acts of the Apostles.

When James Baldwin recalled the terse African-American song about "the fire next time" in the famous essay he wrote some thirty years ago, the flames conveyed an apocalyptic vision. There was, Baldwin was saying then, not much time left. The wounded rage and desperation born of centuries of broken promises, neglect, and racial contempt were approaching the point of volcanic eruption. The fire he conjured in his essay would neither guide nor purify. Like molten lava, he warned, it would cascade from its subterranean recesses and embroil everything in its path. It would not discriminate or make fine judgments. It would swamp and oxidize everything it touched.

What do the fires that raged through Los Angeles in May 1992 on the heels of the Rodney King verdict mean? Can one read anything in them except the fierce eruption from the depths that Baldwin so eloquently foresaw?

For people of faith, all events—no matter how seemingly meaningless or transparently logical they first appear—must be pondered in the light of God's continued presence and activity in human history. The Hebrew prophets not only forewarned the people of what the Creator would do if they continued to violate the covenant and ignore its requirements for justice and compassion. They also tried to help the people discern what the Holy One was doing in their midst. They looked reality in the eye and saw there the mysterious presence of the One who suffers with the wounded, shares the lot of the oppressed, and never ceases to cut down and rebuild the cities of the earth so that even out of the wreckage and embers, a New Jerusalem can arise.

As the sermons and statements brought together in this book testify, God has not left us without prophets in our own age. After the eruption in Los Angeles, indeed while the flames were still leaping, the voices of women and men of faith could be heard urging the people not to despair, surrender to cynicism, or accept uncritically the mass media interpretations of what had happened and what needed to happen next. Rabbis, ministers, and priests, women and men of many denominations, races, and cultures, and from many sections of Los Angeles strove to fulfill the obligation placed upon them to help their people do what prophets, including the prophet from Nazareth, insisted we must all do at such moments—try to discern the signs of the times, to see what the Spirit is doing in our midst and what that same Spirit expects us to do.

The editors of this book are convinced that the words of these contemporary prophets should not be lost to those who were not within earshot when they were first uttered. No ordinary "collection of sermons," these inspired responses to the fires are themselves flames—intense, leaping, piercing, crackling. They draw us in and refuse to allow us to be mere listeners or observers. And this is because they are not crafted by mere observers but by men and women who moved amidst the events they try to help us understand. They are words spoken in the very light of the flickering flames by preachers who, however tongue-tied and numbed they felt by the tumult around them, knew they had to say something, something that would help their puzzled, bewildered, and shaken congregations not to give up on God—or on the vision of an ultimate City of Shalom—because their world seemed to be collapsing amidst screaming sirens, tangled fire hoses, and shattered plate glass. The real test of the preacher or the prophet often comes not when she or he is granted the luxury of carefully honing a sermon in the seclusion of a study on an "average" week (if there is ever any such thing in Los Angeles). It comes, rather, when, with little time to think, one must answer the anguished question of those who ask, "Is there any word from the Lord?"

That question, if not in those words (and most often it was surely not asked in those words) was voiced not just in every quarter of the City of the Angels; it was asked all over America and the world. It rose up from the African-American congregations of South Central Los Angeles who saw their confidence in American justice bruised and kicked beyond recognition. It echoed over Koreatown where newcomers to the city felt themselves wrongly singled out for vengeance. It resonated as churchgoers gathered in Simi Valley, a name once unfamiliar to all but people in the area, but—after the King verdict—now condemned overnight to bear an unsought stigma. The question hovered over Hollywood and Beverly Hills. It haunted the barrios. It was asked in a thousand different ways. It required—indeed demanded—an answer. It could not be ignored. And it was not.

Not a single contributor to this astonishing volume would accept the proposition that words, however inspired or eloquent, are enough of a response to the travesty of the King verdict, the murder and mayhem that followed, or the incendiary conditions that had piled up in Los Angeles—and that continue to pile up there and in countless other cities. Words are obviously not enough. But neither did the authors of these pages give in to the trendy and cynical notion that there is "nothing to say." Nothing to say? Nothing about the awful collage of injustice and abandonment that have brought our nation to this sloping precipice; nothing about the extraordinary measure of compassion and determination it will take to turn us around? Is there really nothing to say?

There is, as Koholeth the Preacher assures us, a time for silence. But as the same prophet of God also says, there is a time for speaking out. The first days of May in the city of Los Angeles were certainly such a time. And these prophets spoke out with power. They spoke, as Rabbi Steven Jacobs spoke, from the pulpit of Calvary Baptist Church, at "a defining moment in American history." They spoke, as the Rev. Linnea Pearson did at the First Unitarian Church in the middle of the ravaged city, "with ashes in our mouths." They spoke, as the Rev. Jesse Jackson put it, "though hearts are heavy and minds confused." But speak they did. And we can all be grateful they spoke. Because, now that the fires have been quenched, and the terrible danger that we will go back to what we were doing before looms over us, we need their words more than ever. We need them in the weeks of sorting out our fears that lie ahead, and in the years of rebuilding we must now undertake, not just of Los Angeles, but of our whole nation. These are words that, though spoken in the heated urgency of the eruption, have an enduring value.

My hope, nourished by reading these words, is that the pall of smoke over the City of the Angels has not obscured the rainbow sign, the promise of peace it betokens, and the covenant with all nations and tribes it signifies. The "next time" of the old spiritual and of James Baldwin's historic essay has, it seems, now come. We need no longer, *can* no longer, wait. The sign has now come. The next move is ours.

Introduction

by Ignacio Castuera

"We must preach with the Bible in one hand and the newspaper in the other" urged professor K. Morgan Edwards, quoting Karl Barth back in 1964. More than a quarter of a century later, many of us in Los Angeles could not ignore the newspapers and all other news media as we prepared our sermons for Sunday, May 3, 1992. Our city had been jolted by a social earthquake as thousands of angry and frustrated people rioted throughout Los Angeles, looting, burning buildings, beating and even killing those who appeared to be different from the attackers.

We were in the midst of Eastertide in the church year, but in the midst of death and destruction in our city. What was the Word of God for this time? This collection of religious responses includes sermons preached in Los Angeles on the Sunday after the beginning of the riots. They are shared with readers around the country because all the preachers firmly believed then and now that the religious community has words of hope, peace, and justice for precisely moments like the ones we faced in May of 1992 in L.A.

The predominant perspective shared here is Judeo-Christian, but we endeavored to share the cultural and religious richness of our city. That which appeared to divide our community, our ethnic diversity, holds also the promise of richness and vitality. So we share out of our faith and culture images of hope from our time and city, hopefully for many times and places where pain and hopelessness of any kind are experienced.

I love the city—not just the one in which I live but all urban existence. Something precious came into being with urbanization, and religious institutions for many centuries coexisted and thrived in urban centers. Industrialization and secularization presented a new challenge to religious institutions in the city. People of diverse ethnic backgrounds flocked to urban/industrial centers with hope in their hearts and minds for a better future.

Religious organizations responded bravely in the early stages by turning churches and synagogues into hubs of activity to assist those who had not fulfilled their dreams, or had them on hold. The "social gospel" in Protestantism had parallels in Roman Catholic social teaching and work, and there were also Jewish institutions operating that were motivated by similar perspectives.

After World War II religious bodies experienced growth, especially in the mainline Protestant churches, but that growth took place as the "suburbs" came into being and the "inner city" was abandoned.

The history of the church I serve is a small mirror image of the history of churches in the city. Built in 1930 by a congregation that had already outgrown two other sites, Hollywood United Methodist Church continued to grow through 1948, when the popular pastor who had led the church, Glenn Phillips, was elected bishop. After 1948 this congregation "hemorrhaged" in spite of the fact that top pastoral leaders were appointed to serve. No one could stop the migration to the suburbs or the new migration of people of different ethnic and economic backgrounds to the core of the city. Like most churches in similar situations, leaders in the congregation spent most of their time bemoaning the loss of white, established members instead of celebrating the arrival of new, younger, ambitious, hardworking people of diverse ethnic backgrounds. By the 1980s this and most city congregations were too small and too scared to be effective in ministering to the constantly changing cities.

I do, indeed, love the city. I was fortunate to be in seminary from 1964 to 1968 when theologians were calling us to celebrate the city and to enjoy diversity. My theological heroes—John Cobb, James Cone, and Harvey Cox— were people who planted in my mind, heart, and soul the idea that differences are to be encouraged and celebrated rather than feared. By the time liberation theology came into the picture, I had already been prepared to accept it as one more of the theological influences that would enrich the church. Alfred North Whitehead, who influenced Cobb, was fond of quoting Latin. One of my favorite quotations from Whitehead is *"E diversitatibus potentia"*: there is power in diversity, or power flows out of diversity. Cities in general, and Los Angeles in particular, are places of diversity and they need to own and believe Whitehead's quotation, especially at times when diversity seems to spell out destruction and chaos.

Two other thinkers that have influenced my perspective on the city are Teilhard de Chardin and Paolo Soleri. Teilhard de Chardin believed that organisms become vulnerable in direct relation to liveliness: the more lively, the more vulnerable. Soleri believes that cities are in fact organisms and that the dictum of Teilhard de Chardin applies to them as well. Modern cities are extremely complex and lively "organisms" that are extremely vulnerable.

Los Angeles can be seen as exhibit one of Soleri's theory. We have an exciting, complex, multicultural center that is also very vulnerable, as the last days in April and the first days in May of 1992 have demonstrated. Los Angeles must also be seen as a microcosm of the whole nation, if not of the whole world. Homogeneous communities are going to be more and more the exception in years to come. It behooves the rest of the nation to view Los Angeles in the same way in which old miners used to look at the canaries they brought into the mines to warn them of dangers. That is one of the reasons our collection of sermons and statements is important. Even though they emerged from a very local event, that event, and the complex causes that precipitated it, affect all urban centers of our nation.

Because our area is so rich in cultural, ethnic, and religious varieties, I endeavored to share that richness in this collection.

It is true that timeliness is important and that one of the guiding principles identifying and organizing the material in this book was the willingness of the contributors to work hard and turn in their documents immediately. But variety is important also, and the people and groups who made contributions were asked to do so because they represented the richness of our urban area.

There were voices that just had to be included. Dr. Cecil "Chip" Murray is the pastor of First African Methodist Episcopal Church in Los Angeles. He and the congregation he pastors have been at the center of African-American life in the city long before the '92 Los Angeles riots. They also became the center of the religious response to the riots.

Much the same can be said about Holman United Methodist Church and their pastor, The Rev. Dr. James Lawson. Jim has been in the forefront of city, state, and national interracial issues for decades now. From his early years in Memphis working with Dr. Martin Luther King, Jr., to the present, Lawson has epitomized the best of the religious response to racism and hate.

We were fortunate to have had Jesse Jackson preaching in at least six sites on May 3. We include the sermon he preached at All Saints Episcopal Church in Pasadena. It was not accidental that this church was selected by Jackson for one of his sermons. The rector of the church, George Regas, and the congregation have distinguished themselves as a courageous group tackling the most difficult of issues confronting the church, including racism.

Father Robert "Bob" Fambrini from Blessed Sacrament Roman Catholic parish was catapulted into fame/notoriety when someone responded to the archbishop's appeal to return looted items to Roman Catholic Churches. Father Fambrini received some looted lingerie from the world famous Frederick's of Hollywood. His picture holding ladies undergarments was published in the *New York Times*. Yet Blessed Sacrament and Bob Fambrini are more famous in Los Angeles for the multicultural nature of their congregation. Fambrini is fully bilingual, having spent several years in Peru, and the parish includes the "Centro Pastoral Rutilio Grande," a center of activities for Central Americans, primarily from El Salvador.

Other contributors are less famous but no less involved in the life of the city. There are many stories that could be told as a way of credentialing them for this collection. The inclusion of their material should in itself be a credential of sorts.

Two Jewish contributions deserve a special introduction. Rabbi Jacobs and Rabbi Rosove lead Reform congregations that have an established record of social concern. Their remarks are included not only because I wanted to share the religious richness of our city, but because these two leaders have distinguished themselves within their faith community and beyond.

Rabbi Rosove's example is particularly poignant. He leads the congregation of Temple Israel in Hollywood. Because of the riot and the ensuing curfew, the Yom Hashoa (Holocaust Day) Observance had to be cancelled on Friday, May 1. On Sunday, May 3, John Rosove and seventy-five members of his congregation went to worship

at the African American Messiah Baptist Church pastored
by The Rev. Ken Flowers. Later they stayed around for
fellowship and work. Vignettes of hope such as this one
deserve to be shared with a nation that has primarily
heard about the horror of the L.A. Riot.

Public Pathos, Private Pain:
A Personal Postscript

In the midst of the public tragedy of a city torn by strife,
the private pain of its citizens continued. Death came
suddenly to almost sixty people directly as a consequence
of the riot. Other slower deaths were also taking place. In
San Diego, David Jessup, who had lived in Los Angeles
most of his life, lay dying of AIDS. From his deathbed Dave
was having more influence upon the world than he will
ever know. Years ago he asked me to preside over his
memorial and I promised I would do it.

The day when the verdict of the Rodney King trial was
shared with an unbelieving nation, a medical verdict was
shared with a loving family and a group of friends: Dave
had only hours to live. The memorial, the family decided,
would have to be on May 9.

I was scheduled to attend the General Conference of
the United Methodist Church in Louisville, Kentucky, but
scrapped my plans when I was informed that Dave would
die soon.

The day I was supposed to leave for Louisville, May 5,
I began to feel the urge to do more about the riots than I had
already done. Several parishioners had urged me to share
my sermon with the larger community, and it occurred to
me that other religious leaders might have had similar
reactions to their presentations. A few phone calls later I
was convinced that we needed to share our thoughts
"wretched from our pain," as Chip Murray told me, at least
with our colleagues in ministry.

A call the next evening to David Polk, a longtime friend
from our seminary days, solved two other problems for me:
Who would publish it? And, was I not some kind of

"vulture" capitalizing on the public pathos of our city? He responded that the press he edits would be very interested in publishing our statements and suggested that the royalties should be placed in a special interreligious fund for reconciliation. My conscience was quieted and the work proceeded. But this work would not have started at all as an idea in my mind had it not been for the fact that David Jessup held me back in Los Angeles. From his deathbed David Jessup gave me, and all who read this collection, a great gift.

*M*aking an Offer You Can't Refuse

Cecil L. "Chip" Murray

The Rev. Dr. Cecil "Chip" Murray is pastor of First African Methodist Episcopal Church in Los Angeles, the largest African-American congregation in the city and the center of the religious response to the conflagration of April 29 through May 2, 1992.

"**J**esus, why did you come to Los Angeles?"

"I have come that you might have life."

"But Jesus, we already have life. Jesus, we've got day life, night life, morning life, afternoon life. We already have life."

"Yes, I see you people are very lively. As a matter of fact, you might say you are incendiary. I spent a few hours in the Simi Valley. Oh, you have life. And I was down to Parker Center. You have life all right, but I have come that you might have a different kind of life."

The Good Shepherd always sentences you to life. The Bad Shepherd always sentences you to death, and the good sheep always know the difference. The Good Shepherd is the one with integrity. The Good Shepherd is the one who is genuine. What's our street language? "Straighter?" Jesus says to each and every one of you this morning, "Baby, I'm for real! If I tell you I love you, I love you. If I tell you the truth, the truth will set you free. If I tell you you are equal in the sight of God, red or yellow, black or white, all are precious in his sight. I want you to believe that. Baby, I'm for real."

Some here think that "coke" is the real thing—both kinds of coke. That's because you haven't met Jesus yet. "Oh, everyone who thirsts, come unto me and drink." Everyone, you don't need money. Jesus paid it all. "If you are thirsty for righteousness, come unto me and drink. If you are thirsty for dignity, come unto me and drink." Jesus is the real thing.

The Bad Shepherd comes always to take life, and the Bad Shepherd comes always dressed as the Good Shepherd filled with words of love. The Sheriff who sentenced us—and really that person is not a judge; down home we used to call him the High Sheriff, and the High Sheriff was a symbol of terror—the High Sheriff gave us a change of venue. The judge gave us a change of venue that took us away from a valley of possibility out into the Simi Valley of Death. I know if I get them out there, they'll do the right thing. I love you. The Bad Shepherd loves all of the sheep, except the black sheep.

And the four great heroes of the West have been through training that said everyone is to be treated with dignity. You are to love everyone within the environs of Greater Los Angeles and you have a club on your side and a gun on your side and the National Guard at your back and the Army, Navy, and Marines waiting to come to your rescue. You don't have to be a bully force. And yet they crucified Little Rodney. "I feared for my life surrounded by twenty armed police persons." Poor Little Rodney prostrate, couldn't even help himself if he wanted to. But they love all the citizens, they love all the sheep. Except the black sheep.

And the jury charged to lift up the dignity of the law—the law of our land given to us by the law of God, the law that's so sacred that when it is absent or vilified we cannot live in peace with each other, cannot live in fairness and equity with each other—those twelve good people and true go into chambers and they sit day after day after day after day and they come out and they say, "We twelve good people and true love all of the sheep and we find these four sheep not guilty. We love all of the sheep except the black sheep."

The Bad Shepherd who wears the badge, the Badge Shepherd who says it's an apparition, the Badge Shepherd who gives a blanket of approval: "I want you to go out to the streets and I want you to love all of the sheep." And then he winks in his Gateway self and says, "Except the black sheep."

Then the sheep get together. The white sheep get together over there because the bad sheep doesn't like a color mix. And then the Bad Shepherd puts the black sheep over here. And the black sheep look at the white sheep and say, "Lord, what's going on? They outnumber us twelve to one. I sure hope they've got fair minds." And the white sheep put their heads together. "What we going to do about them black sheep?" And 50 percent of them say, "Treat 'em fairly." And 50 percent of them say, "Treat 'em poorly."

Are we some aberration? No, here is a radio poll conducted by a radio station represented here today. They polled thirty-three hundred people about the outcome of the Rodney King verdict and they just split almost down the middle. Fifty percent said, "We think it's a bad verdict. We think they brought in an inequity of justice. It was a bad verdict." And fifty percent said, "We think it's a good verdict. They have done nothing wrong." So what we have is a good verdict from a good judge sending it out in a change of venue. A good verdict coming down from a good jury. This good verdict that's good for nothing except creating chaos, pitting us against each other, causing us to hate one another. Good for nothing. Good for nothing.

Jesus, let me show you what goodness is. Jesus, I hope you can count way up into the thousands because I'm going to count every spiral smoke plume that's going up into the sky. Jesus, I hope you can look at the alienation of black against white, against Korean. Every man's hand is set against every other man. Every woman's hand is set against every other woman's hand because of this "good" verdict.

Some shepherds create chaos, and some sheep capitalize on chaos. It's bad enough when the Bad Shepherd mistreats the black sheep. It's even worse when the black sheep mistreat each other. Now, black sheep, you didn't start all of those fires. Every four minutes a fire? My goodness, fires don't move on CPT. (Our precious non-black brothers and sisters, CPT stands for Colored Peoples' Time.) Little black sheep didn't start all of those fires. For the first news reports the northern boundary was Florence Avenue. Then we come up to Slauson Avenue. Then we are at Vernon Avenue. Then we are at Wilshire Avenue. Then we are at Melrose Avenue. Then we are at Sunset Boulevard. And we don't live up there. We work up there. We didn't set all of those fires. When the record is cleared, maybe it will show we didn't set most of those fires. But we do have to confess we did set some of those fires.

To our shame, because now our mother's crying in the ghetto. Because Boys Market had built stores in the ghetto and Boys Market came in along with a few other markets when nobody would return after the 1965 riots. Fifteen of the stores burned down can never open up again because they'll have to build new, and yesterday three representatives of Boys Market came and we sat together in the office and we talked together in the office and we had prayer together in the office. I felt their pain. How could you treat us in the same category as your enemies? How could you treat your friends and your enemies alike? And I have to say we understand that Ted Watkins of Watts Labor Action Committee in South Central has served black folks for a generation. They burned his office down. Golden Bird Chicken is "black bird chicken." They burned his office down. The truth of the matter is, we have no excuse for going around setting fires, for now we have no place where mothers can buy milk for their children. It is in our communities that we have no means, and somebody is gonna have to get a bus transfer and go way up in another section of town, leaving our wealth in that section of town and coming back with nothing but a bag full of nothingness.

We are not proud that we set those fires, but we'd like to make a distinction to America this morning—the difference between setting a fire and starting a fire. We set some of those fires, but we didn't start any of those fires. Those fires were started when some men of influence decided that this nation can indeed exist half slave and half free. Those fires were started when some men poured gasoline on the Constitution of the United States of America. Those fires were started when somebody decided that the very pioneers who started this city should not have freedom and justice under the law. Those fires were started when somebody poured gasoline on the criminal court and the civil court, when somebody took word and truth and poured gasoline on it and burned the whole structure down. But it is not to our credit that in a flicker of those fires we were found looting and robbing and pillaging and stealing, for that is not us, dear hearts. We are noble people. I know a mother can say, "I was stealing milk for my baby." I understand, but why didn't you come to the church? I understand what you were doing, but I cannot condone it.

Baa baa black sheep, have you any wool? Yes sir, yes sir, three bags full. Ham for my belly, booze for my brains, television for my entertainment just in case it rains. Ohhhhh, black sheep!

Black sheep, you must have wool on your head, and you are learning that wool is good wool cause God made it, but God put the wool on your head, not in your head. You have to use your head. You want to be able to say, "I'll go hungry before I'll go humiliated." And before I'll be a slave, I'll be dying in my grave and go home to my God and be free. Choose hunger before humiliation.

You ask, why are the little black sheep jumping on each other? Why? When I was a younger man they made a home brew called "Sneaky Pete." A lot of things go down smooth. Sneaky Pete went down as smooth as Dionne Warwick and Al Green. But once Sneaky Pete went into action, Sneaky Pete would blow the top of your head off.

Sneaky Pete. A hundred and fifty men of the church stand on Western and Adams at 3:00 in the morning, having been there for three hours, standing between fifty police persons who want to do that staccato step, to do that Kent State thing all over again. You could look in some of their eyes and you see, "I ain't whipped, I ain't whipped a black sheep in a long, long time." Not all of them, but it only takes one idiot to make an idiocracy. And on the other end, a hundred and fifty young black men throwing rocks and stones and bottles from the alcohol they had consumed, provoking these people to move forward. And the men of the church said, "No. No. No. Don't throw that." They formed a line, presenting their bodies as a living sacrifice. And what was egging the rock throwers on? Sneaky Pete, a little black sheep with a woolly mind hollering out, "Throw the stone, throw the stone, throw the stone." And what does he have in his hand? Absolutely nothing. And where is he located? Way in the back. So that when the head whipping starts, he'll start. Sneaky Pete.

Well, why would anybody follow Sneaky Pete? Whether he is Western/Adams Sneaky Pete or Parker Center Sneaky Pete, why would anybody follow Sneaky Pete? Why would anybody endure an embarrassment to the City of the Angels, one of the most sophisticated cities in the world, having a little black sheep with a woolly mind talking for everybody? Why would we endure Sneaky Pete?

Go to Israel and watch. The shepherd has the sheep drinking and eating. Then the shepherd calls out "Aaaaaa weeeee" and the sheep get up and they follow their shepherd and he knows the names, "Come on Bill, come on Bloods, come on Crips, come on Preachers, come on." Everybody knows their name and they follow him and someone asks the guide, "Sir, will the sheep always follow the shepherd?" "Oh yes. Except the sick sheep, they'll follow anybody."

Well, I'm coming home now. I just want to tell you about our friend who says, "I'm for real." He says, "I know my sheep. My sheep know me and my good sheep follow me and my sick sheep will follow anybody." And my good sheep, let me tell you this morning, we've got to clean up the town. We've got to clean up the air. And as you clean up, smoke gets in your eyes. But don't you worry about that. Weep a little bit and keep on walking. Smoke gets in your eyes. Blink a little bit because you cannot see through tear-drops. You cannot see through the occlusion of hatred and anger and violence and you'll lump all white folks together. You'll lump all Korean folks together. You'll lump all black folks together. Weep a little bit, but keep on walking and when the smoke gets too thick for you, sit down by the side of the road and have a little talk with Jesus. Tell him all about your troubles. Then remember: Jesus, you brought me all the way. You are such a wonderful Savior. I have never known you to fail me. Jesus, you brought me all the way.

Then you get up and you keep on walking—walking up the King's Highway. And before you know it, there's a warm hand in your hand. There is your Friend who brought you out of the Valley of the Shadow of Death. There is your Friend who fed you when you couldn't feed yourself. There is your Friend who educated you when you couldn't educate yourself. There is your Friend who defended you when you couldn't afford an attorney. There is your Friend who helped you build a house when the bank credit lined your house. There is a Friend. Walk on with him. Walk on by faith. Clean up. The smoke is passing over. Walk on by faith and you'll never walk alone.

In the name of Jesus.

Who Is My Neighbor?

Paul Yung

The Rev. Paul Yung is one of ten ministers of Young Nak Presbyterian Church, one of the largest Korean churches in the U.S. Rev. Yung's responsibilities include ministry to the large English-speaking segment of the congregation.

Luke 10:29-37

Injustice, racism, riot, destruction, looting, and killing— these words were spoken over the radio and television, and these were the words that decorated all of the news reports these past three days. Shock, fear, helplessness and frustration and anger and hostility and more hostility and anger and anger and anger occupied everyone's mind. Rodney King, rioters, the victims, and all the civilians, especially the African-American community and Korean-American community, the old and the young, and all the religious leaders, including myself.

Yes, I confess to you that my heart was full of anger and hostility and anger these past three days, but I couldn't help myself. So I asked—I asked all first-generation Korean Americans, "Why have we come to this place? Why

17

have we come to this country in the first place?" How foolish we were to follow the American dream, and how naive we were to believe in harmony among different races. That much was I filled with anger.

And the Lord God, I think he heard our prayer and I think he heard our cries. And our Lord Jesus gave this text to me when I was preparing for the sermon because I had to change the topic of today's sermon. We originally planned for the Friend Day, reaching out for each friend to believe in Jesus Christ and to celebrate together the friendship. It just was not the right time to do that because there was too much suffering around us, and the Lord God gave to me this text, this parable of Jesus Christ.

As we all read together this afternoon, a man was traveling down from Jerusalem to Jericho and he was robbed. He was stripped, he lost all the things that he had. He was seriously wounded. He was lying down by the side of the road helpless, just grieving. I am pretty sure his heart was full of anger and hostility. "What did I do wrong? What did I do to you that you beat me so harshly? And you took away all my possessions and you almost killed me."

Just like the lawyer who came to Jesus and asked this question, "Who is my neighbor?" so I ask the question, "Who is my neighbor?" This is a time that I want to draw the clear line, and my anger tells me I don't have to deal with the people I don't want to deal with anymore. I want to draw the line just like the lawyer asked. He was asking a question. What is the definition of my neighbor? He wanted to come up with a rule and draw the line and just dwell within the boundary. I was just like that. And Jesus gave us the parable just as he gave to the lawyer a parable.

There was a man robbed like you, beaten like you, and almost murdered like you. A priest passed by, a Levite passed by, but they didn't care for him. Later a Samaritan passed and he stopped and he took care of him and he took him to the inn and he promised, "If you will take care of this man, when I come back I will pay all of the extra expenses." And he left him with this promise.

You know, I have preached this passage many times before, and I have also heard sermons on this text several times before. And every time I heard this passage and message, it always condemned me, because I was just like the priest and the Levite, just passing by because of the heavy schedule, because of all the duties that I had to carry out in the church. But this time was different. This passage gave me comfort instead of a guilty conscience. This passage gave me hope instead of frustration. Why? Because there was no choice. I had to be identified with the person who was robbed. We are the ones beaten without knowing any reason. We are just traveling along this life and we are robbed all of a sudden. We are beaten harshly. We are here helpless, and that is why this text became a passage of comfort and new strength.

In our church, more than thirty families became victims of this riot. One family even lost their son who was just eighteen years old, who just grew up and became an adult and now he is gone. He was running toward a Korean store to help them defend their store right in the middle of the exchange of shooting. He was killed.

In our Korean-American community, there are many families who came here fifteen, ten years ago and now they have established one business, ready to go on, to move on, and all of a sudden it is completely burned down. They don't know what to do the next day. And Jesus told us this parable. In all the parables of Jesus Christ there is anticipation of the kingdom of God through the life of Jesus Christ. So in this parable we see that Jesus himself is the true good Samaritan. I didn't realize that before, but in this passage the Lord is just doing the same thing as the good Samaritan. As I was crying out to the world, as I was identifying myself with this robbed man, I suddenly realized that the good Samaritan was Jesus Christ himself, and this message all of a sudden turned to become a message of comfort and strength and hope.

Now let's turn to the passage again and see what the good Samaritan did.

Verse thirty-three says that a Samaritan, as he traveled, came to where the man was, and when he saw him he took pity on him. He didn't simply pass by, but he took pity on him. Our Lord Jesus does not simply pass by our sufferings. He takes pity on us. Not just us, but all the people who are suffering in the midst of these riots. The Lord Jesus, who promised us that he will be with us to the end of the age, is here with us right now. He is in the midst of the burned down structures, right above the ashes where the families gathered and cried. He is there because he takes pity on them. And then he said he went to the wounded man. He went to this man and bandaged his wounds, pouring on oil and wine. Then he put the man on his own donkey. Why? Because this man was helpless. He couldn't walk anymore on his own strength. He needed help. Knowing that, this good Samaritan carried this man on his donkey all the way to the inn.

That is what our Lord Jesus Christ does for us right now. He knows that many of us are helpless. We cannot move on anymore with our own strength so he decides to carry us, so that we can move on. And then he promised, "Take care of this man. When I come back, I'll pay all the extra expense. I'll pay you back everything." That's the promise that the Lord gives us today. Are you the victim of this riot? Are you suffering from the loss of your business and family members are wounded? Listen to the promise of the Lord. "I'll pay you back."

Don't just put your pride first in the midst of your sufferings. We all know that we became helpless and I believe that this is the time that we just cry out to the Lord, "I cannot go on. I am weak. I lost everything. I need your help." Just as to the robbed man lying down at the side of the street and grieving and crying for help, the Lord listens, and he will come and take pity on us and come right beside us, knowing that we are helpless, with no strength at all. He will carry us to the place where we can be healed. "I promise I'll pay you back."

I want you to notice here. The good Samaritan, when he came to this robbed man, did not say anything judgmental. This road from Jerusalem all the way down to Jericho was a notorious road. It was known for being a dangerous area. No one who knew the area would dare to pass by after the sun set. And the scholars tell us that the road had a nickname: the "blood road" or the "blood way." But this good Samaritan came to this man and didn't say, "Didn't you know that this is a dangerous area?" He just took care of him and did his best to bring the healing.

Just like that, our Lord Jesus Christ comes to us. He will not say, "Didn't you know that the kind of business that you had, that's where the most crimes are happening?" Not all Korean Americans lost their businesses because they did business in the crime area, the dangerous area. But the Lord didn't say anything about that. He simply came. Without rebuking, he provided the care and healing. That's our Lord!

And this story reminds us of what the Lord said in many different places. "In the world you will face tribulations, but take confidence because I have overcome the world."

I would also like to read a scripture text from Romans, another promise that comes to us from the apostle Paul. It says:

> Who will separate us from the love of Christ? Will hardship, or distress, or persecution, or famine, or nakedness, or peril, or sword?...No, in all these things we are more than conquerors through him who loved us.
>
> Romans 8:35,37

The Lord Jesus Christ who loves us is right beside us, right next to us, saying, "I promise I'll take care of you. I'll bring you to the healing and I'll pay you back."

When I was able to identify myself with this robbed man, new strength and hope began gradually to replace the anger and hostility that was in my heart. And I began to ask once again, "Who is my neighbor? Who is my neighbor?"

And Jesus told this lawyer, "Which of these three, do you think, was a neighbor to the man who fell into the hands of the robbers?" And the lawyer said, "The one who showed him mercy." And Jesus said, "Go and do likewise."

Right here Jesus is saying: "You ask me a question because you want to draw a line—Who is my neighbor?— but I am saying to you, you don't need any more rules and you don't need any more laws. What you need is just to go out and help those people who need your help. Whoever needs your help is your neighbor!"

In this text, there is no information. Jesus didn't say anything about the cultural or racial background of this robbed man. Jesus just said a "man" was robbed. And Jesus is saying to us who are asking, "Who is my neighbor?" "Don't ask any questions about their racial background. Don't ask any questions about their cultural background. Don't ask any questions about why they got into that environment, and don't ask any questions about how you and each person are involved in this riot. All you need to do is just to go to the people who need your help and be a neighbor rather than asking, 'Who is my neighbor?'"

I was shocked when I got a phone call from my father-in-law who lives right at the corner of Western and Sixth, right behind the shopping mall that was completely burned down. He said that the shopping mall had caught fire. "We have to escape right away, so can you come down and help us?" I picked up two of my nephews and we drove down to the apartment. The shopping mall was already burning out of control, but there was no fire truck. We went to the apartment and found out that everyone in the apartments was evacuated. My mother-in-law has been suffering from cancer for the last two years. She can't move at all. She cannot even go to the restroom. She has been bedridden for a few months. There was nothing she could do on her own. Fortunately, several young men helped us to carry the mattress with my mother-in-law on the mattress all the way down and out to the street and put her on the back of a pickup truck. When I got there and I saw this thing, I was shocked. It was a battlefield, such a tragedy. We carried her back to the Glendale area where we live.

So I said, "Okay, this is my neighbor, my family, my relative." But the Lord Jesus doesn't want us to draw the line there. He asks us to expand the line beyond that level. The next day I came to church and we began to have the reports from church members. Some lost their businesses; some lost their properties. One family lost their dear son, Eddie Lee. As I was getting all of these reports, I said, "Okay, these are my neighbors, my church members, and I'll help these people." But the Lord Jesus didn't want me to draw the line there. He challenged us once again to expand the line.

The same afternoon, I decided to drive around Koreatown, the Korean-American community. Boy, if you have been there, you know what a war is like. Most of us have never been to a battlefield, but you go out there and it sure must be like that. And I said, "Okay, this is my community. Now I'll draw the line here; I'll pray for my community, I'll help my community, I'll gather with my brothers and sisters and restore this community." But Jesus challenges us once again to expand our line of boundary. He demands us not to ask any questions about our racial background, not to ask any questions about the cultural background, not to ask any question about how each of us was involved in this riot. Jesus is telling us that we are all losers. Nobody is a winner. We are all losers of this social evil. So he asks us to go in unity, not just for our family, not just for our church, not just for our community, but to go to everybody, everyone who needs our help, who is the victim of this riot, and be a neighbor to them.

I believe that this is the time that we should be united. United, not to condemn others, but united to care for others. United, not just to defend ourselves, but united to restore our community and rebuild our city. United, not just in hatred and hostility, but to replace the hostility and anger with love and forgiveness. United for the peace and justice and unity beyond all races and all cultural boundaries, beyond all the rights and wrongs. Only then, can we truly begin to build justice and peace and then the city.

You all know that this city, Los Angeles, is covered with darkness. This reminds me of a story about a rabbi who was asked the question, "Teacher, how could we tell that the night is over and the new day is coming? Could it be when we see an animal from a distance and can tell whether it is a sheep or a dog?" And the rabbi said, "No." "Could it be when we see a tree from a distance and can tell whether it is a fig tree or peach tree?" And the rabbi said, "No." "When is it then?" And the rabbi said, "It is when you see the face of your brother and sister in every man and woman. Otherwise, no matter what time it is, it is still dark. A new day is not coming."

I believe the streets of Los Angeles will be cleaned up in a few days. I believe that the Korean community will build the community again, no matter how long it takes. And I believe somehow our African-American communities will restore their areas, but it won't matter unless we look into their faces and can tell that this is my brother and sister. It will still be dark, unless we look into the face of a white man and woman and say that's our brother and sister. Unless we see the face of a Latino and say that's our brother and sister. Unless we can see the face of anyone and say, "You are my brother or sister," it is still dark. A new day is not yet coming.

So the Lord challenges us: "I am your neighbor, I'll take care of you. Now I want you to go and be a neighbor to others without asking any questions, but simply providing things to meet their needs. Be a neighbor."

We all know that this is Children's Sunday, according to Korean tradition. Little children have seen many things they are not supposed to see, at least not yet. Now it is time that we, the grownups, show to them what they must see. Show to them that love overcomes the hatred. That love overcomes the violence, and that love can rebuild and love can create a harmony among many different races. And only love will last forever.

Remarks in the Wake of the L.A. Riots

Rabbi John L. Rosove

Rabbi John L. Rosove is the religious leader of Temple Israel. This address was delivered at Messiah Baptist Church on Sunday, May 3, where Rabbi Rosove and seventy-five members of his flock were guests in the heart of the devastation.

Pastor Flowers, thank you for your graciousness in giving me these few moments to speak to your congregation. All of us from Temple Israel wanted to be with you today. Our growing friendship with you these past two years in our Covenant Relationship has meant a great deal and continues to bring us closer to one another. For our friendship, I thank God.

My heart is heavy as I speak to you today. Not only have these riots shaken our community's sense of safety and security; but, also, yesterday I learned that Howard Epstein, the son of one of our synagogue families, was murdered on Thursday at the beginning of the rioting. He was here from Orinda where he, his wife, and his two small daughters (ages nine months and seven years) were living. He had

25

come to check on his business and to be sure his seventy-five employees (African-American and Hispanic) were safe. He had rentèd a car at the airport and had journeyed to South Central L.A. where his business was located. While stopped at a light, three men pulled up alongside him and shot him dead. They didn't know that his employees loved him. Nor did they know that, despite economic hard times, Howard could not lay off his employees because they were his friends.

After services this morning, I will be making a condolence call to his parents' home, a task that breaks my heart. Howard's memorial service is scheduled for Tuesday at Temple Israel.

So much has transpired in so short a while—a wake-up call, if you will, not only to the people of Los Angeles but to the country as well. The Rodney King verdict strains credulity, but anyone with any understanding knows that this was the tip of the iceberg. The rage we saw so violently exploding in the streets must be condemned for its viciousness and lawlessness by all decent people. But the feelings of despair, alienation, and anger cannot be ignored. Not all the looters are criminals, though much of it was, no doubt, opportunistic theft. When a mother of five children remarks that this was the first time she was able to put shoes on the feet of all her children, then we have to wake up to the reality of the lives of far too many people.

Pastor Flowers and I spoke on Thursday morning about how extraordinary the Rodney King verdict was. And I told him that so many white people simply do not understand the lives of black people in this part of the city.

Last January, Pastor Flowers invited me to participate in the city-wide celebration of Dr. King's birthday at McCoy Memorial Baptist Church. I was, along with City Attorney Jim Hahn, the only white face in that church. I had never in my life been in that neighborhood. I felt very much the minority and not a little out of place. But I was proud to go and be with Pastor Flowers and others whom I have come to know here at Messiah. I must tell you that only since getting to know you folks at Messiah have I begun to understand what your lives are about, about your dreams and about the nature of your community. I have grown to appreciate who you are and respect you as I had never known before. And I consider myself enlightened, empathic, and openhearted.

The people in Simi Valley haven't the foggiest idea about the realities of what it means to be black in a white world, at the hands of certain white police who've lost control and displayed vicious animus toward indefensible black people.

This is why their verdict went the way it did. We need more understanding between black and white, more economic empowerment in the African-American community, more opportunities for business investment and more black ownership of businesses, a higher voting percentage, more political power, and the building of coalitions of decency between black, white, Korean, Christian, Jew, Muslim, and all peoples of faith.

If better conditions, better lives, and greater understanding come as a consequence of these riots, then we can say "dayenu" (it will have been enough!) But much work needs to be done in the months and years ahead. We need political leaders with courage and community leaders who speak the truth. We need the effort of every black, white, and Asian person living in this community. And we need goodwill and the willingness to take risks and make sacrifices for the common good. For purposes of enlightened self-interest, this is a necessity. In the interest of God's will, it is mandatory.

God bless, and may peace come to us soon based in justice and greater mutual understanding. Amen!

*O*ut of the Ashes: "A Terrible Beauty Is Born"

Linnea Juanita Pearson

The Rev. Linnea Juanita Pearson is pastor of the First Unitarian Church of Los Angeles, one-half block east of Vermont Avenue in the heart of Koreatown.

This morning we come together with ashes in our mouths. We come with anger in our hearts. We come with aching in our bodies. We come with bitterness and mourning.

Come, let us gather together, out of despair, desolation, and death. Out of darkness, desperation, and doom. Out of loneliness, separation, and alienation. Out of agony and fear, let us gather together in our tears and in our pain.

Come, let us gather together again. Let us gather up the ashes, and blow upon the embers until a fresh spark ignites to give light to the life that is yet to come, that we might gather around this new fire of hope and warm ourselves.

I want to say, first of all, to those of you who have been worried about our waterfront, that the armed National

Guard is out patrolling the beaches with their rifles at the ready. So those of you who have been worried need not be so. No one can steal our sand or our polluted ocean waters.

I learned, as many of you did, only yesterday, that President Bush was calling out five thousand Marines to come into the city. I was wondering why he was calling out the Marines after the worst of the destruction has been wrought. Then I learned that he was coming to town on Thursday for a trip he planned long ago, a political visit having nothing to do with the riots. Clearly he's scared.

So the Marines have landed in Los Angeles. But to be honest, he's not the only one who is scared. We've all been afraid these last, long, three and a half days. And we still are. For we've seen our so-called civilization shaken to its roots, almost uprooted. Almost completely overturned. Dissolved. By Friday night all of us, even the most anti-militaristic among us, were wondering when the National Guard was going to arrive, and why were they not put into position until after the worst of the violence had been unleashed.

It was prescient, I think, that in our service last Sunday, commemorating the Holocaust and the Chernobyl meltdown, several of our new members spoke of their experiences of coming out of the ashes in their lives, when they felt that they, or everything in their lives, were dying or being destroyed. They told of their experience of rising out of that time, often supported by one or two friends or a small community that gave them new hope.

Today we are literally surrounded by ashes. We have no choice but to try to find the spark of new life coming to birth within these ashes, and within ourselves. It is either that or capitulate to the forces of death and destruction.

I want to reflect with you today on the events of these last three and a half days, first on the level of societal structural analysis, and secondly on the level of psychological and spiritual introspection.

The societal structural analysis is easier and less painful, for it presents a more objective and less personal approach to the disaster that has engulfed all our lives these last few days. On this level we can see the struggle in relatively simple terms as one between the haves and have-nots. But even this level of analysis is neither comfortable nor pleasant.

We might begin with the verdict that came down on Wednesday afternoon from Simi Valley, and we might note that the jury that pronounced that verdict was a jury of the peers of the accused officers. It was not a jury of the peers of Rodney King. And, as so often happens in rape cases—and Rodney King was in a sense raped by those officers of the law—in such a trial the victim becomes the accused, and the verdict of the jury essentially is determined by the attitude that "he or she asked for it."

This is the way the oppressor class always justifies its oppression, whether it is of Nazis against Jews, whites against people of color, men against women, heterosexuals against homosexuals, the rich against the poor. Or it is peoples of the so-called "First World" against peoples of the so-called "Third World," Croatians against Serbians, English against Irish. "They've asked for it." This is the verdict the non-Afro-American society generally has put on the Afro-American society: "They've asked for it." They've asked for their poverty, their oppression, and their second-class citizenship.

Why is it a surprise, then, to find the "they" revolting? Those who identify with Rodney King: the poor, the oppressed, people of color, rising up with a loud angry roar and saying, "No! No more! We won't accept this. We've had enough. We won't take it anymore." And why is it a surprise that this all began in the age-old manner of an "eye for an eye"? It was on some deep primitive level that the first violence that began three and a half days of retribution was the beating of a white man by an Afro-American man in a manner that paralleled the beating of the Afro-American Rodney King by Euro-American cops. This was a not unnatural regression to the "eye-for-an-eye" mentality, and it was no coincidence that it followed only two weeks after the powers and principalities of the state of California had endorsed this "eye-for-an-eye" mentality by the execution of Robert Alton Harris. If the state can take blood revenge, why not the people?

Of course, in the saner moments of our collective consciousness, we know that if we live by the law of an eye-for-an-eye, we will end up with a society where everyone is blind—speaking figuratively, not literally, using blindness as a poetic metaphor, not as a physiological condition, for we have among our membership those who are physiologically blind, and they, like the ancient blind sage, Teiresius, are often gifted with deeper insights and vision than the many of us who are sighted.

On this level of societal structural analysis, I've been amazed by our media-appointed social commentators and government officials—including, and especially, President Bush—who have told us repeatedly over the last few days how they have been puzzled by the violence and by such sights as women and children, whole families, looting ransacked businesses and stores. I have wondered how these self-appointed spokespersons could not make a connection between this grass-roots violence and the violence of the upper echelons of our society: a society that has over the past four decades spent trillions of dollars building up a doomsday arsenal of mutually assured destruction, hoards of nuclear weapons that could wipe out all life on this planet. And even last week it was planned to explode yet another nuclear device in the deserts of Nevada. Ours is a society based on violence, extinction of the indigenous peoples, and a bitter system of slavery. As Malcolm X said, "Violence is as American as apple pie."

And the so-called "bad elements" in the poorest echelons of our society are but mirror reflections of the "bad elements" in the richest echelons of our society, those who have been running our country for their profit for over a decade. To those who question those poor people who seem to just "be taking advantage of the situation," I say: "They have learned well their lessons from the super-rich."

And thus the barbarism, destruction, and violence we have witnessed here this last week is but a tiny fraction of the barbarism, destruction, and violence the United States government has wreaked upon the world in this last decade.

How is it then that these self-appointed media commentators have missed commenting upon the hypocrisy of a government that condemns lawlessness in the streets while condoning and exporting lawlessness abroad: the mining of the harbors in Nicaragua; the torture and death squads in Guatemala, El Salvador, and Chile; the invasions of Panama and Granada; the bombing of Libya; and the genocide in Iraq, slaughtering over one hundred fifty thousand innocent men, women, and children?

How can they not see the moral contradiction between our nation's congressmen and congresswomen cashing millions of dollars in bad checks while a poor person cashing a ten dollar bad check goes to jail? Is it any mystery why the rage of the poor is so intense and volatile?

How is it that they fail to make the connection between a President who, not wanting to be a "wimp," draws a line in the sand, setting in motion Operation Desert Storm, and a gang leader who marks out his turf with graffiti on street corners?

How is it they fail to make the connection between the spontaneous, anti-establishment violence we have witnessed these last few days in the streets of L.A. and the violence perpetrated by such establishment groups as the N.R.A., whose ads on TV feature old Moses himself, Charlton Heston, and whose lobby is so powerful as to disallow even the most mild gun reform laws?

How is it that our President and our media have missed the news that the poor have been getting poorer and the rich richer through governmental policies guaranteeing social inequities, and that this sort of institutional violence cannot go on forever without a rawer sort of violence breaking out in the streets? How is it they have missed the hypocrisy of a President and a government engaged in multi-billion dollar cocaine and armament trading, while condemning the nickel and dime dope peddlers on street corners selling a few brief moments of drug-induced bliss to poor and desperate people who cannot afford a bottle of

Don Perignon, a health-club membership, or a trip to Hawaii to help ease their stress and escape their misery?

Where is the outrage at these governmental violations of all that we hold honorable and true? Where is the outrage at a national government of international gun and dope dealers that mirrors its outrage on two-bit dope dealers and ghetto gang leaders? Where are our contemporary prophets, our Micahs, our Isaiahs, our Ezekiels who will call out to our nation's rulers "SHAME!"? Where is our modern-day Lincoln who can proclaim that our nation cannot continue to exist half slave and half free? Or three-fourths slave and one-fourth free?

Where are the leaders brave enough to proclaim that we cannot tell Eastern Europeans that capitalism is going to work there when it doesn't work in our own inner cities? Or in our rural areas? Or even in our suburbs? Where are the social commentators who will see the sin in a society that condones the crass commercialism that fills our airways with ads for overpriced luxury goods and then condemns the desires aroused in an under-employed and unemployed populace that knows they can never afford these goods, and thus takes what they can when the getting is good?

Where are the prophets who will make the connection between the spectacle on CNN yesterday of thousands of poor and unemployed standing in lines before the South Central L.A. post office for their welfare checks and the carefully crafted ad for BMWs that followed that unseemly sight? Where are the prophets who will call to task a Texas oil millionaire President who has supported a multi-billion dollar S&L bailout but deplores poor families taking this opportunity to bail out Pampers and Coca-cola and motor oil from their ransacked neighborhood stores?

I have been appalled at how these self-appointed, well-paid social commentators have failed to make the connection between the greed that has swept away the moral fabric of our nation in the last decade—the junk-bond scandals, the corporate raiders, the closing of American plants to find cheaper labor in foreign lands, the tax system that has allowed the top 5 percent of the population to amass wealth equal to the remaining 95 percent, the multi-billion dollar national debt—and the hunger of the poor people pushing shopping carts loaded with grocery store loot across asphalt parking lots and pot-holed streets to fill their empty home larders.

In the words of the late Malcolm X, "The pigeons have come home to roost."

James Edward Olmos referred to these events as a parallel to the Boston Tea Party, the start of a new American revolution. But he failed to note that, in this case, the occupying power is not the foreign-based English, but the American Marines, the National Guard, and the LAPD, and their firepower is much greater than that of the rebels. And the rebels are not organized, have few leaders, and no one to speak for them in the halls of power.

How then can we respond to this? How as a church community can we begin to respond creatively in the midst of all this chaos? How can we be a voice for the voiceless?

Surely one proper response to the chaos and cacophony is a time of silence, of hushed contemplation, a time to enter into a deep self-and-other reflection. For the truth is, we know in our heart of hearts that we are all both the victim and the victimizer, the oppressor and the oppressed, the violent and the violated.

And before any healing can take place we must come together in our common human brokenness and woundedness, confess our personal and communal sins, and ask expiation and forgiveness of one another and of that great Creative Power through which we all are bound together in one shared creaturehood, whether we call that power "Indra's Net," "the mystical body of Christ" or, in Unitarian Universalist terms, "the interconnected web of all existence."

And what better symbol of that common human brokenness than the pained face of "the criminal" Rodney King on the front page of today's *L.A. Times*? And does that face not call to mind the face of another "criminal," called Jesus of Nazareth, who also bore the lashes of the police and the soldiers who were the occupying forces of his land and who, as armed protectors of the state, like the LAPD, did not allow that any should question their power?

This Rodney King is the man portrayed to us by the police as "an animal," "a brute," a "gorilla in the mist." This is the man who took fifty-six baton blows in eighty-one seconds "to be subdued," this is the man who had curses hurled upon him, this is the man whose broken and bruised body we saw bloated and disfigured days after the attack, stunned and beaten into silence and submission. And we saw him on CNN yesterday, barely able to hold back his tears, his face contorted in agony, crying out, "People, I just want to say...can't we all get along? Can't we get along? Can't we stop making it horrible for the older people and the kids? We've got enough smog here in Los Angeles, let alone to deal with the setting of these fires and things. It's just not right....We'll get our justice....The truth will come out....There'll be a higher court this thing will go to.

"I love everybody. I love people of color....But we've got to quit....We've got to quit...to keep going on like this...to see a security guard shot on the ground...it's just not right...these people will never go home to their families again."

And then this Rodney King, beautiful in his blackness, powerful in his brokenness, poignantly shared with us his dream—not so different from the dreams another King shared with us before he was assassinated—"I would want to help people who had law enforcement problems. They'd get up and they'd have a job to go to every morning. All kinds of different jobs. I'd have some of them cleaning up the community. I do love green, seeing that green, seeing green yards. So I'd have some plant trees and clean lawns....

"And, I mean, please. We can get along here. We all can get along. We've got to, just got to. We're all stuck here for a while....Let's try to work it out. Let's try to work it out."

So now, having seen this beautiful, broken man appeal to us in this gentle manner, how can we say "no"? How can we fail to respond to his call for us all "to get along"? Surely we, as a church community, must, following the words of Rodney King and Martin Luther King, and that Jewish prophet of old who was mockingly called "the King," try to work it out, because, "we're all stuck here for a while."

And as we come together in our common broken humanity, with tears and anguish in our eyes, we might see come to pass what the poet William Butler Yeats saw in the aftermath of the Irish rebellion of 1916. "A terrible beauty is born," he wrote (*Easter, 1916*). Yeats saw his Irish countrymen and countrywomen transformed in the anguish of struggle with their British oppressors, transmute anguish from simple, easy-going, lackadaisical peasant-folk into men and women of power, the power that comes from within, the power that cannot be broken by the sword or the whip or the rifle of the state, the power that comes from living one's life for justice's sake and the "terrible beauty" of a Martin Luther King, Jr., or a Malcolm X, or an Aung San Suu Kyi, the Burmese woman freedom fighter presently incarcerated by her government and the most recent recipient of the Nobel Peace Prize.

And in this "terrible beauty" that is born from the juxtaposition of love and agony, of hope and despair, of faith and fear, we here today might also find the source of our deliverance, the seeds of our redemption, the synergy of our collective souls seeking earnestly to overcome evil with good, and in the words of the prophet Isaiah, we might come to "loose the bonds of wickedness, let the oppressed go free, share our bread with the hungry, bring the homeless poor into our own house, and not hide ourselves from our own flesh."

And perhaps it will come to pass that, in this sharing of our common humanity, in this coming together in our common brokeness, in this "terrible beauty" of our shared love and pain, we might see, to paraphrase the words of Isaiah 58:8, that our light might break forth like the dawn, and our healing spring up speedily.

And out of the ashes of our despair we might see arise the phoenix and the phalanx of a people united, flesh of one flesh, heart of one heart, soul of one soul, a rainbow creature of many colors and sounds shaking out its brilliant plumage to amaze and comfort the afflicted and afflict and redeem the comfortable.

And then, as we busy ourselves to clean up the mess made by the fires, we might also find the way to clean up the mess that made the fires.

I am suggesting six specific ways to begin this process:

1. We will immediately begin emergency food distribution to persons in this area.

2. We will coordinate volunteer efforts with other disaster-relief centers in this area.

3. We will send out teams of listeners to each of the major ethnic groups within a five-mile radius of the church to hear their problems with the LAPD, the INS, government agencies, the schools, the gangs, other ethnic groups, etc.

4. With this collected data we will decide how we can respond both to the immediate needs and injustices and to the need for fundamental social change.

5. We will develop and begin to execute a several-tiered program of long- and short-term action to do what needs to be done.

6. We will find the funding and personnel to do it.

And then shall justice flow like a pure river, even through the once-polluted Simi Valley court system, and righteousness like an everflowing stream, even through the once putrid halls of our nation's capitol, and the vales will be exalted and the hills shall be made low, and every woman and man and child, 'neath their vines and fig trees in South Central L.A. and all around the world, shall live in peace and be unafraid.

For we know, finally, that we must love and serve one another or die. Let this be our vision. Let this be our way. Amen and Amen.

*H*ow Have You Helped Me?

Chester L. Talton

The Right Reverend Chester L. Talton is Suffragan Bishop of the Los Angeles Diocese of the Episcopal Church. His message was delivered at a regional celebration of his body at Christ the King Church in Santa Barbara on May 9, 1992.

Matthew 25:31–46

Jesus is responding to his disciples' question: what will be the sign of your coming and of the end of the age? He responds with several parables, among them this one about the judgment of the nations, or the separation of the sheep from the goats.

It has never surprised me that those who are welcomed into the kingdom are those who gave food and drink, who welcomed the stranger, who took care of the sick, and visited the prisoner. What did interest me was that Jesus identified with those who were in trouble so intimately as to say, "Truly I tell you, just as you did it to one of the least of these who are members of my family [brothers and sisters], you did it to me" (25:40).

The people divided as sheep don't remember when they did these things for Jesus, in the parable, but when you

39

reach to help those who cannot help themselves (the least), the word from Jesus is *you help me.*" Likewise, those divided as goats say they do not remember when they failed to help people who were in trouble, and the Lord says, "Just as you did not do it to one of the least of these, you did not do it to me" (25:45). *Go away from me!*

In my imagination I stand before the Lord making an accounting of my life and work at the end of the ages, and I recount all of the good things I believe myself to have done. Terror strikes my heart when I imagine that the Lord will ask me what I did with the opportunities given to me, to serve the "least."

"I made you a bishop in my church, Chester. How did you use the position, the influence and power of that office, to serve those who were in trouble? Did you speak for them to those in power? Did you stand with them? Did you try to empower them? Did you actively seek to reconcile my brothers and sisters with one another? Knowing as you did how I am one with those in need, did you speak for them?

"When I was born in Watts and in Compton, did you care that I was taken home to a two-room apartment with linoleum to cover the floor? Did you call my mother lazy because she was on welfare? Did you care that my school district spent one half the amount on each classroom as was spent in many suburban school districts? Did you care when I received my high school diploma and could still not read or calculate?

"When I came to the United States undocumented and you saw me standing on the corner waiting for you to drive by and offer me work at pay far below what you know I need to subsist, did you care? When my family came here from Korea and moved into the only community where we could begin business, to a community of deprivation shared with those who could not get loans to begin such a business at all, and resented us because we did get a meager amount together, did you care when we clashed, when we fought over the crumbs that fell from your table? I tell you, just as you did not do it to one of the least of these, you did not do it to me."

We have all been through an ordeal this past week as we heard first of the verdict in the case of the four Los Angeles policeman accused of using excessive force in the beating of Rodney King. I was stunned with disbelief when I heard that they had been found innocent on all counts. It was difficult to believe because I knew that people all over the world had seen with their own eyes, as I had, the police beating this man beyond what the situation warranted. Surely this time, with such proof of brutality, the police would be found guilty. But the jurors had seen this excessive treatment with their own eyes, over and over, and they still denied what they saw. I was shocked, surprised, stunned. What this said to me was that a black person could be beaten nearly to death, before the eyes of the world, and the agressors not be punished for it. It was certain proof that black people are not regarded as human beings worthy of the same safety and protection other citizens receive.

I was saddened by the explosive response that came from South Central Los Angeles, but I was not surprised. My hope that justice would be served and that equality before the law would be lifted up was dashed. I am a middle-class black, but I was disappointed and I was angry. It did not then surprise me that those black persons who are poor and who are under-educated, who have no hope for a better life, would explode. Why not? What do they have to lose? I think that it was meant to say: "Look! Pay attention, those of you who have power, and who benefit from power! We are here and we are human! And if we can't live, you will not live comfortably! The police are killing us. We will not suffer alone!"

African Americans and Koreans should not be at odds. What we should do is come together, and the Spanish-speaking should be part of this. We do not have real power—we are all struggling, we should not be enemies fighting over fewer and fewer crumbs that fall from the table of the privileged. We could have *real* power if we could come together and insist on having an equal place at the table when decisions that affect our lives are made.

We have experienced great pain over the past week. Our people have lost their businesses, their jobs, their homes. Our hearts have been heavy and the sorrow great. Yet, in the midst of this, we are hoping against hope. We are talking—we are reaching out to help in the short-term. Let us begin together to build structures for the long-term. There is unfinished business in this country; it started before the Koreans or Hispanics became an issue. But all of us must work out the solutions.

Jesus is poised now, again, to ask the question: "How have you helped me?" We have another chance. We believe that Jesus is the African American—the Korean American—the Hispanic American—the Anglo American, trying to reach out, and struggling to come together.

We need fundamental change. Those who have privilege must be prepared to give it up and to share what are limited resources. If we would respond to Jesus, we must see Jesus in the "least of these" so that we can hear the call we long for and need: "Come, you that are blessed by my Father, inherit the kingdom prepared for you from the foundation of the world" (25:34).

Safe on Broken Pieces

Jesse Jackson

The Rev. Jesse Jackson, prominent political and civil rights leader, preached at six different churches on Sunday, May 3. This sermon was delivered at the Rector's Forum at All Saints Episcopal Church in Pasadena.

Acts 27:40–44

"So they cast off the anchors and left them in the sea. At the same time they loosened the ropes that tied the steering-oars; then hoisting the foresail to the wind, they made for the beach. But striking a reef, they ran the ship aground; the bow stuck and remained immovable, but the stern was being broken up by the force of the waves. The soldiers' plan was to kill the prisoners, so that none might swim away and escape; but the centurion, wishing to save Paul, kept them from carrying out their plan. He ordered those who could swim to jump overboard first and make for the land, and the rest to follow, some on planks and others on pieces of the ship. And so it was that all were brought safely to land."

Some of us are more able to swim than others, and some get on boards, and the rest in some ghetto or barrio in some faraway place, and some on broken pieces of the ship. So it came to pass that they escaped all safe to land.

This morning, in that our ship has wrecked at night and is in flames, I want to make the appeal to you to be part of the command to make it on broken pieces. To make it on broken pieces.

As we meet this morning, America's promise is being tested. America's authenticity is being tested. America's character is on trial, and though hearts are heavy and minds confused and disappointment abounds, remember: whom the gods would destroy, they first make mad.

Some swam, some on boards, some on broken pieces. What we saw this week was a kind of spontaneous combustion. After all, that is simply accumulated, discarded materials, ignited by friction or some spark. You cannot have spontaneous combustion unless there is a lot of discarded material that has been discarded for some period of time. What we find in urban America and among forsaken farmers are discarded people, and now for several generations we have watched them smoke and finally explode.

Beyond the troops, trying to bring some measure of order and stop the burning and the maiming and the killing, beyond the Justice Department coming in after the fact to address the behavior of the police, now what? The Bible teaches that without vision the people perish, but happy is he that keepeth the Lord. We've got to see our way out. The Rodney King beating was the caboose on a long train of abuses and were it not for the video we would not have believed Rodney King's testimony. The jury would not believe it and they saw the video. They were so deep in their resentment and their foolish ways, they not only would not believe Rodney King, they would not believe their own eyes.

We see a people neglected, rejected, and then humiliated by another miscarriage of justice. It's not just Rodney King. The Attorney General said to us Thursday morning they have prosecuted 128 cases of police brutality since 1988. It's not just Rodney King. It's young Phillip Penell, a young African-American teenager shot in the back by two white policemen and killed while other police sold T-shirts celebrating the work of those police, and they walked away free. It's not just Rodney King. It's Don Jackson, a policeman right here on the coast, being thrown through a plate glass window, and that was on camera. It's not just Rodney King.

Jackie and I have been blessed to have three well mannered sons who, I can say without fear of contradiction, neither drink liquor nor engage in drugs nor carry weapons. Jesse Jr. will finish law school a year early this December after finishing seminary two years ago. Jonathan finished Northwestern Kellog School of Business after both he and Jesse graduated from North Carolina A. & T. Ucell will graduate from the University of Virginia this year in May, a year early. And yet all three of them have looked down the barrels of police guns and had handcuffs on their wrists. "Looked dangerous"—young black males at risk.

When that last happened to Jesse, he had just graduated from college and we bought him a car for graduation. He was going to the Pancake House, had not put the window sticker on yet. Two police pulled him and his classmate over. "Get out, say nothing, just get out. Hands on top, spread eagle, get out, say nothing." Handcuffs on— get in back of car—"we'll take names as we drive you to the police station. Where did you get this car?" And at some point one of the police, while writing down the names, said, "Now state your name again." This was one week after my family's appearance on television at the '88 Democratic convention. He said, "Jesse Jackson, Jr." He said, "Him?" Jesse said, "Yes." One policeman said, "Oh hell." The other one said, "It does not matter. He goes with the wagon." At risk.

The Kerner Report showed that never did pure poverty explode into a rebellion. It was always Newark or Detroit or Chicago or L.A. It was always an act of police or community friction, always some slave master's whip or stick or gun where insult was added to injury. The Kerner Report showed us the danger of two Americas, one essentially black and brown, one white.

Today Germany spares nothing to close the gap between West and East Germany so as to have one nation. The risk they run of having an upper West Germany and a lower East Germany is ultimately rebellion and civil war, and so they invest in lifting East Germany up, not lowering West Germany. They see the wisdom of one nation.

As I walked the streets of Watts, I saw lots vacant since 1965. I saw the grandchildren of those who rebelled twenty-seven years ago. The Kerner Report has been ignored—Kerner disgraced and arrested. Amazingly, with all of the burning, the property loss is about a half billion dollars. That's a half billion too much, but one of the payments on the S&L bailout is twenty-five billion dollars. If they just missed one S&L bailout payment, you could usher in a whole state of hope and vitality to urban America—just one payment shift.

Let's look at this combustible material. The number one cause of death for black males between fifteen and forty-four is homicide. Twenty thousand three hundred fifteen young black men killed between '78 and '87. Guns were involved 78 percent of the time, but—discard them. The homicide rate among black males rose over 65 percent in the last five years; 95 percent of the rise is due to killings by guns, but—discard them. Today in some areas of the country it is more likely for a black male to die from homicide than it was for a U.S. soldier to be killed in Vietnam, but—discard them. Blacks are 6 percent of the nation's population, 3 percent of the college population and 46 percent of the prison population, but—discard them. In New York, there are forty-five thousand black males in prison or on parole and that's double the number enrolled in college, but—discard them. Nationally, 23 percent of black men in their twenties are in prison or on probation or on parole, but—discard them. Between 1976 and 1986, it is estimated that the number of black males in college decreased by thirty thousand. The odds of a black student entering college within ten years of graduation from high school are less than half the odds of a white student. The arrest rate of black males in the U.S. is four times the arrest rate of black males in South Africa. In the U.S. the arrest rate for black males is 3100 per 100,000 to South Africa's 729 per 100,000. Discard them.

And so, when you get through discarding them, the throwaways, this is the stuff with which the combustion is made. Stage one: ignore the problem. Stage two: active humiliation. Stage three: chaos. Stage four: the troops are in. Quietness. But quietness is the absence of noise. Peace is the presence of justice. The combustible-materials conditions must be removed. We need alternatives to the alienation.

Pain abounds in the nation. Four hundred thousand defense workers laid off in California—those who did all the right things, degrees, veterans, engineers—now competing in unemployment compensation lines. Ten million Americans unemployed, twenty million jobless, one of every twenty-five on welfare, one in every ten on food stamps, thirty-five million in poverty, forty million have no health insurance. Unlike the stereotype, most black people are not poor and most poor people are not black. Most poor people are white and female and young. But, whether white, black, or brown, hunger hurts. A baby goes to bed at midnight. It does not cry out in race or sex or religion. It cries out in pain. In church somebody must love all the babies, just because they are babies. Don't stop there. Most poor people are not on welfare. They work every day. They raise other people's children. They work every day. They drive cabs. They used to make cars; they drive cabs now. They work in fast-food restaurants. They cut other people's grass. They wipe our bodies in the hospitals when we are sick. They empty the bedpans, the slopjars—no job is beneath them. And yet, when they get sick, they cannot afford to lie in the bed they have made up every day.

Now with this pain abounding we must choose partnership over polarization. We are at what one might call the critical mass. It's just not welfare. That's picking on the most vulnerable. Welfare recipients are not closing American businesses. They're not raising tuition. They're not taking family farms. They're not taking medical or legal slots in schools. They're not trillions of dollars in debt.

Welfare is the exhaust pipe of the system. Let's look at the engine. The top 500 corporations have not created one new job in ten years. And they've lost market share and job share. Market share and job share goes down, welfare goes up. It's called the same system. And while they've lost job share and market share and failed at being competitive, guess what? They got bonuses. And when the plant collapsed they strapped on golden parachutes to leap out and land on soft grass. Is it really about welfare? U.S. foreign held assets: eight hundred billion dollars. Receipts: five hundred billion dollars. Taxes on the receipts: three billion dollars. Economic strip mining.

I slept in Imperial Courts and Nickerson Gardens, in the heart of Watts. I talked with 50-percent-unemployed black youth, 25 percent among the adults. Three generations of children with crushed dreams. They have no dream of a health insurance policy. They have no dream of entering college. They have no dream of owning property. No dream of owning their own house. The infrastructure for their downfall is greased.

A child goes to the youth correctional center in downtown L.A. for a year and it costs $34,000. A child goes to Dorsey High for a year, $5,000. Cal State L. A. for a year, $6,000. You spend six times more per year to jail a child than to educate the child. Many of those youths want sweet grapes of hope and not dried bitter raisins of despair. But going to jail is a step up, a step *up*! They jump up and touch the basement. They are way down. What's there in jail? They will no longer be hit by drive-by shootings. Once they're in jail the AK47s and uzies that they buy and rent in L.A. are locked away. Once they're in jail it's warmer in the wintertime. It's cool in the summertime. Once they're in jail they have adult supervision and organized recreation and balanced meals and trade training. They have everything in jail that, if our priorities were correct, they would have where they live. We've got to change the course.

The riot is not a plan or a strategy. It's a reaction. The evidence is, though they were humiliated by their Rodney King verdict, not one juror has been inconvenienced. I stood in the line yesterday at 83rd and Vermont and watched seniors standing there for six and eight hours to get their checks. Standing there without johns, places to relieve their bodies. Old people unable to hold their water. Standing there six and eight hours! Then, when they got their checks, the currency exchange had been burned up. The grocery store, burned up. Once they got their checks the drugstore, where they get their medicine from, burned up. The service station to get gas, burned down. They can't catch a cab—the drivers won't come into the war zone. They go home, lights out, refrigerator off, food spoiled.

Riots represent, as Dr. King once said, the voices of the unheard. It's like when those who should speak, don't speak. And those that ought to cry out don't—and then, ultimately, the rocks cracked. Rocks don't have eyes. They don't have a sense of conscience. They're just hurled though space.

We must urge a partnership today. We must search deeper than we have searched as we fight the spiritual demons that eat away at our souls. This racism, anti-Semitism, Asian-bashing spirit, must go. We need healing. In 1939, nine hundred Jewish people, mostly women and children, got on a ship headed for America, called the *St. Louis*. They got within eyesight of Miami beach, where they were turned away. There was room in the country for the nine hundred Jews but not room in our hearts, and so some tried to swim to Cuba and they were drowned, and others went back to Germany and they were killed.

It was anti-Semitic and wrong to lock the Jews out in 1939—let the record show that. But because the spirit was sustained in 1942, one hundred twenty thousand Japanese Americans were put in concentration camps right here in this country, in this state. Taken from their churches, their schools, their property. But very few analyze that because the spirit of Asian bashing, the demon, prevails. We celebrated young Kristi Yamaguchi winning the Olympic skating medal a couple of weeks ago. Her mother was born in an American concentration camp. Let us look at ourselves. While the Japanese Americans were going to these camps because of these stereotypes and backhand swipes, the most decorated fighting unit at the end of World War II was the Nisei fighting unit. Even while their parents were being humiliated, they were dying that we might live. Wasn't it anti-Semitic and wrong to lock the Jews out in 1939, and racist and wrong to lock the Japanese up in 1942? Isn't it also racist and wrong to send the Haitians back to Haiti in 1992, and to abandon urban America?

What are we going to do about it? When it's dark and the lights are out you can't use color for a crutch, because all of us look amazingly similar in the dark. Plants closing, farms auctioned, corruption in high places, explosions in low places—what do we do when it's dark?

First, admit that it's dark. After twenty blacks had been killed with choke holds, a police chief suggested that it was applied because blacks had strong necks. And that was tolerated? It was darkness. Three days after the Rodney King beating was on television, *three days* after it had been on TV, Mr. Bush had police chiefs come to the White House. He invited Daryl Gates and pointed him out as an American top cop hero. Three days after the beating was on TV. Those are not points of light. Those are shades of darkness in high places.

It's dark. In high places. When it's dark, admit it's dark. When it's dark, don't adjust to the dark. Don't surrender your life. Don't surrender your dreams. Don't surrender your aspirations. Keep on believing that you can make it and make a difference. Yes, you were born in the slum. Yes, like Jesus was. And perhaps homeless, just as he was born to a homeless couple. Just because you were born in a slum does not mean that it was born in you. Don't adjust to the darkness. Pursue that Ph.D., that law degree, become a justice of the court. Be a teacher that teaches for life, not just for a living. Don't adjust to the darkness. Don't use drugs or liquor as an anesthesia for your pain, because neither drugs nor liquor will bring light into darkness.

We have more today than just a problem. We have a condition. Politicians can solve problems. If you're homeless and they give you a house, that solves that problem. But you get in the house and kick doors down, that's a condition. If you're denied the right to marry, that's a problem. You're permitted to marry by law—that solves that. Your marriage can't stay together because you're not mature enough, that's a condition. If you're denied the right to go to a school of your choice, that's a problem. But to get there and refuse to study and choose to put dope in your veins rather than hope in your brain, that's a condition. That requires healing. That requires an alteration in wants, priorities, and values.

What on earth can we do? Build bridges! That's why I reach out to you today, to build bridges. What must we do? Try and tame the power. What must we do? We live in the same boat and the ship wrecks and the storm is raging. What must we do? There are more available Resolution Trust Corporation buildings, S&L bailouts, than businesses lost in Watts. So maybe, just now, there can be a fair distribution of those assets.

What must we do? Organize a massive registration drive. Fight back! In California, Wilson beats Feinstein by two hundred fifty thousand votes, but guess what? There are two hundred sixty thousand high school seniors in this state, everyone of whom should come across that stage in May or June, with a diploma in one hand and a voting card in the other. Here college students are protesting rising tuition, but guess what? There are 2.4 million college students in this state. With just a 25 percent increase, that's six hundred thousand new voters. What are they going to do about it?

Japan looked like Watts fifty years ago. They had something called the Marshall Plan. Brought them aid, trade, credit, loan guarantees, debt forgiveness, and long terms. Well, I want them to do the same thing to rebuild urban America. While we must build up our allies and not become isolationist, there must not be another dime that goes to rebuild Eastern Europe and Russia without investing in America. It's just basics.

Stop all this foolishness of bashing Asians. That's not right. And it's not accurate. Why is Japan strong? There's nothing mysterious about that. The Bible says, the people without vision will perish, and happy is he that keepeth the law. One of the laws is the law of regeneration, the law of reinvestment. If a honeybee were here and extracted nectar, it wouldn't just fly away. It would drop pollen, and then fly away. Because the honeybee knows by instinct that if it does not drop pollen where it picks up nectar, the flower will die. And when the honeybee grows empty and it comes back: dead flower, dead honeybee. It feeds the flower that it robs. It honors the law. Notice there are no slum honeybee hives. Notice there are no homeless honeybees. There are no honeybees burning crosses in front of other honeybees' hives. There are no American honeybees flying to Japan asking for a break. Because the honeybee obeys the law.

Why are the Japanese strong? Whatever deal we have with them, we cut it from a position of strength. We say, "We won, you lost." Yes sir. "We are big guys, you are little guys." Yes sir. "You cannot have them in Japan, we can have them all over the world." Yes sir. "We make big stuff: MX missiles, B1 bombers. You make little stuff: chips and radios, televisions and cars." Yes sir! Now we got all the big stuff. And no market for it. We're the best in the world at making what nobody's buying.

Why are the Japanese strong? They reinvest in Japan. That's basic. Why are they strong? They educate their children. They send them to schools. They go to school eleven months a year. They pay their teachers at the level we pay doctors and lawyers. They have their most disciplined minds teaching their children. While they learn several languages we picket for English only. Why are they strong? They have a ten-year plan. One hundred million people rebuilding their infrastructure—their roads, their bridges, their sewers. Three hundred billion a year. We have a ten-year, three trillion dollar plan, defending them while they do it.

Why are they strong? While we sent a man to the moon to get some dust and rocks, and come back, the Japanese built a train that goes four hundred miles an hour. If we built the same train—and we can, rather than fire these defense workers, retrain them and convert their skills; rather than close these military bases, use them as re-training sights—we could build a train that goes from New York to L.A. in eight hours while we lay the beds and make the steel and lay the tracks and put America back to work. That's the alternative to welfare and despair. That's the way to make America feel whole again.

We can! And we don't! That's why the church's role in this is critical. We have a crisis in character in high places. Our character is on trial and we're failing the test. Well, how do you measure character? By how you treat the least of these. How do you measure character? Inasmuch as you've done it to the least of these, you've done it unto me. How do you measure character? By how you treat the children and those in the dawn of life. By how you treat the poor in the pit of life. By how you treat the old in the sunset of life. By how you treat the stranger on the Jericho road.

How do you measure this thing called character? One day a man was walking down the street tending to his business. He was jumped, and beaten nearly to death. The priest, the reverend, the rabbi, busy going to his institutional church or temple, Bible and hymnbook in attaché case, saw him bleeding, and crossed to the other side and wouldn't look back. Another man came down the street and approached the man, saw he was from his own race, and said "my brother" and kept stepping. Another man of another race and a different religion stopped! Helped him out! Helped pay for his recovery! It's about character. If our character is right, our resolve to be better will make us better.

The basis of a new national health plan is that people are sick. One day a woman who had the AIDS virus or a cancer or some issue of blood—that's what AIDS and cancer are all about—heard about the Master coming to town with a healing message. She did not have the right to vote, she didn't have the right connection or occupation, and we didn't even get her name. But she had the will to get well, she had faith that God had the power. She reached through the legs of the more ablebodied and she touched the hem of his garment, and the Bible suggests that by her faith she was made well in his power.

When I was a little younger I wondered why Jesus did not stop and give that woman some attention. Well, the more I thought about it, he had already given her restored health. Maybe I want a little too much. Maybe if he had stopped and looked in her face, he might have asked a series of demeaning questions. What's your full name? What's your middle name? How long have you been sick? Are you really sick? Why did you crawl over here? Why are you sweating so much? Are you still married? Where are your children? What is your man's place of employment? What church do you attend? If I heal you, what will be your payment plan? She could have died on the interrogation!

And so today I call you to act, to reach out, to build bridges, to have mercy, to care, to have some human feelings, to see the terrible cost economically and morally of discarded human beings. Reach out, for your own humanity is measured by how you reach out. If my people will call my name and humble themselves and pray and seek my face and turn from their wicked ways, the Bible says, then they will hear from heaven and God will heal their land. It's about character.

On this note, I leave you. Sometime ago I was speaking at a school down south and saw an unusual scene. A six foot eight athlete walked across campus holding the hand of a three foot midget or dwarf. I tried to act as if it looked normal but it didn't. I kept looking back and they kept walking. He was looking down grinning, she was looking up, grinning. And they got to where the sidewalks cross and he picked her up and they embraced and kissed and he gave her her books and she went skipping on down the sidewalk. He went in the other direction.

I said: "Now, Mr. President, I can't contain this. What am I looking at?" He said: "Well, you see, I thought you would ask. He was a top athlete in the state. A four-letter man. That is his sister. As a matter of fact, that is his twin sister. And by some freak of genetics he came out the giant; she came out dwarfed. She did not grow. He was offered a scholarship to the big schools around the state and a pro contract to play ball. He said: 'I will only go to your college if my sister can go.' They said, 'According to the NCAA rules we can not give two scholarships.' He said: 'If she can't go, I can't go.' And somehow we were able to get him because we were able, at this small school, to offer them each a scholarship."

Somewhere he learned this character lesson—that all of us cannot be six foot eight. Some are born short of stature and opportunity. Some of us are born seemingly with a tail wind pushing us down the road while others have the wind coming in their faces. You're not judged by how far you can jump, but by how far you can reach back. He measured his strength not by leaping but by lifting. It's about character.

If we care, we'll be a better nation. Never bitter, always better. Pasadena and Watts, lock arms. Make a new California. Make a new America. I know you can if you will. And you must. You just must!! Amen.

We Are an Easter People

Barbara P. Mudge

The Rev. Barbara P. Mudge is vicar of the Episcopal Church of Saint Francis of Assisi in Simi Valley. She preached this sermon to that congregation on May 3.

John 21:6

"He said to them, 'Cast the net to the right side of the boat, and you will find some.' So they cast it, and now they were not able to haul it in because there were so many fish."

"Were you there when they crucified my Lord?
Were you there when they crucified my Lord?
Oh-h-h-h, sometimes it causes me to
    tremble, tremble, tremble.
Were you there when they crucified my Lord?

I have thrown caution to the winds this morning. My prepared sermon based on this Gospel lesson is now scrap paper. I am angry. I am frustrated. We have crucified the

57

Lord...again. Nothing excuses the violence of these past few days except the continuing crucifixion of our brothers and sisters in the inner city. We are as much a part of what is happening as if we were setting fires ourselves.

Thursday morning I awakened with such a feeling of shame. I did not want to be the vicar of the Episcopal Church in Simi Valley. I was embarrassed by what was being said about the "ethos" of Simi Valley. Throughout the day I received telephone messages from all over the country asking how I was holding up under the barrage of media overkill about Simi Valley. I was somewhat surprised that people were concerned about me while there were so many other mitigating problems to address. People said they were praying for me. I realized that I needed all the prayers I could get, if I, indeed, was going to gather my congregation and be their leader during this tumultuous time.

I decided the first order of business was to hold a service that evening. I asked three people to start telephoning the people in our congregation and ask their presence at a service of evening prayer. I went into the church and started arranging everything for a "decent and well-ordered" Anglican service of evening prayer. It was while I was moving the lectern to the middle of the aisle that I realized that the paschal candle must take primacy over everything else. I do not have answers but WE ARE AN EASTER PEOPLE and that is how we must present ourselves to the world, and so the candle was placed in front of the lectern from which we would read the Holy Word of God to a fractured and confused world. There already had been nine deaths reported. I placed nine red votive candles on the altar. An hour later, I placed four more candles on the altar. By 7:15, when the service was to begin, I had placed another four candles on the altar. My heart was heavy and I mourned the deaths of innocent people, and yet, out of crucifixion must come resurrection.

Our diocesan bishop has already set a plan in motion to help the members of the eight Episcopal congregations that have been impacted by the rioting. He needs money, lots of it, if he is going to be able to help these people get back on their feet. Twenty-two persons showed up on Thursday evening, and those twenty-two persons contributed over $700 for the Bishop's Discretionary Fund. All of you here this morning are going to be given the opportunity to contribute to the Bishop's Discretionary Fund. We are going to take up three offerings today. We shall take up a first offering, and then we shall take up a second offering, and then we shall take up a third offering. The first will be our regular tithes to the church; the second will be for the United Thank Offering, and the third will go to the bishop.

Let's look at the text from this morning's Gospel lesson.

"'Cast the net to the right side of the boat, and you will find some.' So they cast it, and now they were not able to haul it in because there were so many fish."

Once I had cast off my feelings of shame and come to terms that we were an Easter people and that Simi Valley was filled with Easter people, it was up to us to prove to the folks downtown that we in Simi Valley were just as devastated by the events that had taken place as anyone else. Most of us were horrified by the Rodney King decision. But, these riots were not spawned by just the Rodney King trial. This was the spark that ignited a long string of injustices, frustration, and racial oppression. On Friday I learned that two hundred fifty people were being housed at the AME Church on Harvard Boulevard and that they were in need of Pampers, baby food, formula, baby clothes, and blankets.

I called the person who runs our outreach center for needy mothers and babies. She went to our treasurer and got a check for $250 with which to buy the expendable supplies needed. On her way to the bank, she passed a senior swim meet at Rancho Simi Park, and stopped her car, got out and went in and passed the hat. Those fine people responded with donations of $258. At the bank, the teller threw in another $10. Some $500 worth of goods were purchased and put together with clothing from our outreach center and delivered by four members of the congregation to the stricken area on Saturday. The manager of

Von's Market found everything that was needed, cleaned off the shelves when stocks were gone, and gave a discount on the items purchased. This woman, our own Judy Tice, lowered the net on the other side of the boat and came up with a full net. She has never done anything like this before, but she was so intent on helping and improving the image of Simi Valley, that she cast pride to one side and went into that swim meet and fleeced those kind folk for a just cause. We have close to $1000 to send to our bishop. I would like to send at least $2000 from this mission congregation in Simi Valley.

This morning's epistle lesson tells of the conversion of Paul. May I suggest that what must happen to each of us is that our hearts must be seized and converted. This must not happen again. I remember the Watts riots and the hope that things would change. But things have not changed. Those of us who live in nice houses with decent incomes are part of the problem, and we had better become part of the solution. The welfare system in this country must undergo some radical changes. We oppress people and maintain the ghetto mentality by handing out checks to the unemployed instead of subsidizing those who are willing to work at lower paying jobs so that they can begin to feel some sense of dignity and worth. As long as we encourage unemployment we shall continue to oppress. Our education system needs some work, and our mindsets need some work. We need to stop talking about "them" and "us" and start talking about all of the people of God.

I understand the mentality. My father was from South Carolina. When I was in the first grade, my father thought he might find better work if we moved from Southern California to South Carolina. So off we went to South Carolina in the spring of 1937. I was immediately enrolled in the first grade class in the school my father had attended with the same teacher who had taught him. We were staying with my father's mother. One morning, as I walked to school, I struck up an acquaintance with a black girl about my age. We kept walking until we were one block from the school, when she announced that she went to

another school on another street. We said goodbye and
went our separate ways. By the time I reached home that
afternoon, word had reached my grandmother's ears that
her granddaughter had been seen walking and talking
with a black child...only they called them *niggers*. I was
severely reprimanded and told that Covingtons did not
cavort with niggers. My six-year-old heart did not understand, only that I had somehow done something to offend
the Covington name.

We returned to Southern California three weeks later,
but I never forgot that incident, or the one that took a
Japanese friend of mine out of my sixth grade class in early
1942 and sent her off to a "relocation center." She returned
to south Pasadena sometime after the war, and graduated
with the class a year after our graduation. To my horror,
Tyoko was using a wheelchair, the result of having polio
while in the terrible conditions of those so-called relocation
centers. I felt such a sense of corporate guilt. My country,
the American people, had done this to my friend, simply
because she was Japanese and her family's presence on the
west coast might prove a threat.

It was the church, the Episcopal Church, that helped
me through that very idealistic time in my life. We confessed our corporate sense of guilt in the General Confession every Sunday morning, and somehow that eased the
burden as I promised to make sure nothing like this would
ever happen again...and it has...over and over again.

But, older and wiser now, I know that God is present as
we go about the killing and arson. God is present and it is
God that we annihilate, or think we annihilate. God does
not die; God is alive. God may be present on the gallows as
we pull the lever, but God will not be cast out. God will not
be cast out because God gave the one and perfect gift for all
of humankind in the life, death, and resurrection of Jesus
Christ. And so, my brothers and sisters, in the midst of this
chaos, let us show the world that we are an Easter people;
that we have picked up the cross of Jesus Christ and get on
with doing whatever needs to be done so that we do not
keep on crucifying our Lord. Lift high the cross so that it

shines through the smoke and misery and becomes the shining light of a people who do care for one another and love one another as Christ has loved us.

*C*atholic Christians of Los Angeles, Do You Love Me?

Robert A. Fambrini, S.J.

The Rev. Robert A. Fambrini, S.J., is pastor of the Church of the Blessed Sacrament, Hollywood, California, a congregation that ministers to a significant segment of the Central American community in Los Angeles.

ast Monday morning I left Los Angeles for a meeting of priests in Albuquerque, New Mexico. What a lovely time to visit the high desert! The city's weather reminded me much of Los Angeles: hot and dry during the day, with cool evenings. Albuquerque is such a quiet city compared to Los Angeles. Their traffic jams are almost nonexistent, and it was so quiet around the hotel, I felt at times as if I were in a library!

Springtime gives all of us a surge of new life, even in places like California where we do not have much of a winter. Springtime coincides with our time of Easter, and our celebrations are renewed each year with the reading of the resurrection stories from the Gospels.

There are certain characteristics to these stories, certain traits that are often found in the verses: the physical reality of the resurrection, the importance of the passion and the cross, the need to go out and to share the good news.

During these past two weeks of resurrection stories, my prayer and reflection have centered in on the disciples and their reactions to the news that Jesus had risen from the dead. In last Sunday's Gospel we found the disciples huddled in the upper room. Were they gathered in prayer? Were they celebrating their unity as believers? Quite the contrary: they were gathered together out of their fear of the authorities. They were a fearful bunch.

In another place we have the story of the disciples on the road to Emmaus. They relate to Jesus their own deep discouragement about the death of this man in whom they had placed so much hope and trust. They were a discouraged band.

In almost every account, including today's Gospel lesson, Jesus is not easily recognized. There is much confusion as to whose stories should be believed, who has really seen the Lord. Confusion and doubt are ever present. During the days following the resurrection, the disciples had to separate the reality from their own fear, discouragement, confusion, and doubt.

I don't think it was an easy transition. I believe there were times when it was hard, if not impossible, for the disciples to believe that YES, he had risen from the dead as he promised he would.

The fact of the resurrection kept pulling them back to reality. In last week's lesson, Thomas doubted that Jesus had risen, but then fell obediently before his wounded Lord. Today we see Peter, perhaps a discouraged Peter, going back to fishing, the first time we have evidence of this since he initially left everything and followed the Lord. He and his fellow fishermen do not at first recognize Jesus. Then they eat with him, and then there is the painful encounter of the Lord and Peter.

For your prayerful consideration today, in light of the tragic events of these past four days, let us consider the disciples.

Since Easter Sunday, just two weeks ago, our lives have been touched by events that have left in all of us more a taste of Holy Week passion than of Easter joy. It was on Easter Tuesday that we witnessed the first public execution in this state in twenty-five years. The very next day, an event that took place many miles from here affected the lives of many persons in our community: the tragic explosions in Guadalajara. That same evening we even experienced an earthquake.

And now, more sorrow, more anguish, more pain, more division.

We have reason to doubt as the disciples did, to be confused, to fail to recognize him, to respond as Thomas did when told by the disciples that they had seen the Lord: "Oh yeah, where?"

We gather here this morning to pray for peace, to pray for the victims and their families, and to look for signs of hope. But if we are really serious about rebuilding this city, we will experience the same pain Peter felt when asked by Jesus three times: "Do you love me?"

Catholic Christians of Los Angeles, do you love me?

Yes, Lord, you know that we love you. We have such a long history here of our faith in you, dating all the way back to the missions.

Then remove from your hearts any sign of bitterness and hatred for your fellow man or woman. Begin by examining your own prejudice, bigotry, and racism—that tendency within all of us to put our own race first. Check your attitudes about Jews, lesbians, and gays, the homeless and the immigrant among you. To paraphrase the letter from John: "If you say we are not racist, we make the Son a liar and his word is not in us." This is the way you will feed my lambs.

Catholic Christians of Los Angeles, do you love me?

Yes, Lord, you know that we love you. Look at our beautiful churches and see how they are full every week. See our school in which we try to pass on the faith to our children.

Then respect life above all things. A society that condones the taking of innocent life in the womb and the state-sanctioned execution of its criminals can only expect a response of violence from its citizenry. Lack of respect for human life begets violence. Respect of property rights comes only with respect for human life. This is the way you will tend my sheep.

Catholic Christians of Los Angeles, do you love me?

We are discouraged and hurt because we have been asked for the third time, do you love me? It is from that place deep within, that place of vulnerability, that we respond: "Yes, Lord, you know all things. You know that we love you."

Then be your brother's and sister's keeper. If you want peace, work for justice in all things. This begins in small ways—patience behind the wheel while stuck in traffic, concern for the issues that affect your neighborhood and your city, desire that all partake in an equal share of our limited resources. In this way you will feed my sheep.

My brothers and sisters, the road ahead is long and painful. The vibrant spirit of the 23rd Olympiad of only eight years ago and the more recent festive occasion of the marathon in March when all of Los Angeles came out to celebrate are but faint and distant memories now. It is time to weep and be sorrowful, a time to mourn because the Los Angeles of last Sunday has died and will never be the same.

In conclusion, let us return once again to our resurrection stories. We have seen where the disciples were fearful, confused, doubtful, and slow to recognize the Lord, and yet Jesus continued to appear to them. He continues to appear to us, in the midst of the burned-out shell of a city. Our challenge is to find him and for this reason we gather for Eucharist, the very Bread of Life and Hope.

May the Eucharist we celebrate this morning be for us the comfort and hope on our journey toward rebuilding a new city that respects the rights and dignity of all its people.

*F*rom Where Will the Answer Come?

Rabbi Steven Jacobs

Rabbi Steven Jacobs is the religious leader of Temple Shir Chadash—The New Reform Congregation in the San Fernando Valley. His message was delivered at the Calvary Baptist Church in South Central Los Angeles on Sunday, May 3.

This is a defining moment in American history. This is no singular event that is going to go from our midst. The voiceless—however critical we may be of them, in looting and tearing apart the city—the voiceless have spoken and are now being heard.

This is a defining moment in our lives, for me personally as a rabbi—one who can no longer be invited to a black church and get up and talk about brotherhood and sisterhood and speak platitudes and then leave and say we had a nice time together. We've got work to do, brothers and sisters! We have an opportunity and a marvelous challenge to build bridges and to prevent the bridges from being destroyed anymore. The answer to our problems (they are our problems collectively), I believe, will not come from a charismatic leader. The answer will come from you and from me and from us doing significant work together, doing our part in the greater whole, and bringing meaning to our lives and to our children's and to our grandchildren's.

The answer will come from you and me breaking down the stereotypes. It will come from our children who will learn together, please God, and break bread together, and not just see each other in schools where your children and grandchildren are bussed and we treat them as mere visitors. If we are not just visitors in this church, then your children cannot be just visitors in those schools.

The answer will come from each of us as we begin spelling out what hurts us. It will come when we begin to be honest. It will come from each of us, especially if we, as white people, understand, after the Rodney King verdict, that there is great pessimism in the black community about justice in America. It will come as we get to know each other as human beings who hurt, who bleed, who laugh and who have fears and who need the love and understanding that fills this service today.

It will come when we acknowledge that, in America, black means fear to most white people. The fact is, we don't know you as brothers and as sisters. I know, because I realize that just as white Americans by and large fear blacks, I'm told numbers of Americans distrust Jews. *I* know that hurt, and *you* know that hurt.

We've got a job to do, and the answer will come when the President of this great nation means what he says, and doesn't just utter words. When George Bush speaks about his peace dividend, I think we should *demand* a peace dividend. If the Cold War is over, I want the peace dividend in this city and in other cities in the great urban centers before they're all blown up before our eyes. When the President wanted $500 million to bail out the S&Ls, he got it overnight. When he wanted to finance a terrible war in the Gulf, he got it overnight. We want the peace dividend.

The answer will come from people who are involved in building the future of our children and grandchildren. I have never seen this city more galvanized for action than it is now. It will be a long, arduous task. But it's going to take more than just good feelings. It requires an openness in our lives to see how we need one another. There is an apartheid here in America that we have to do away with. Together we have to have a short-range plan and a long-range plan in order to build together. It will go beyond the food pantry. We've got to stop blaming the welfare system and stop placing the problems of the country on the backs of the poor. The violence of the hatred must be stopped.

I believe in tomorrow. These are not just words. I believe we have the power to make tomorrow different from today. I believe that poverty need not be permanent, and that men and women need not learn war anymore. I believe in humanity despite all that we know about human nature. I believe that there can be a time of peace, of shalom, and a time of justice; a time of brotherhood and sisterhood; a time of tranquility for all who live on earth.

I believe that we can share in bringing that day closer by the way in which we live and hold on to one another and touch one another and hug one another and kiss one another. In the words of our tradition, "May the source of peace send peace to our sorrowing hearts, and may we taste the brilliance of godliness in this church and in our synagogue, and may it spill out into the streets of our community."

Our love will persevere. And thank God for people like your pastor, and for all of us here together. May God bless you.

*B*reath from the Four Winds

Ignacio Castuera

The Rev. Dr. Ignacio Castuera is pastor of Holly-wood United Methodist Church, and the one whose thoughtfulness and unflagging energy led to the collection and publication of these sermons.

Ezekiel 37:1–14; John 21:1–14

It happens all the time: we select the scripture readings weeks ahead, because I preach from the lectionary. For several months, we have known that we were going to have this scripture reading from the Gospel of John. The scripture reading from Ezekiel was selected by our Worship Committee. The Ezekiel text was selected because we wanted to celebrate Native American Sunday today and because both Native Americans and Ezekiel refer to the breath or Spirit from the four winds.

In the United Methodist Church we have been blessed with the presence of many ethnic groups, and we like to emphasize these ethnic groups. Today we were going to do a Native American Sunday. We had contacted a group that was going to do a dance of the four winds precisely because we were going to use Ezekiel and this wonderful text of the spirit—the breath from the four winds. Yet something else happened this week, and the whole Native American Sunday had to make room for us to ponder what has happened in our city in the last few days in the light of the good news of the gospel.

Here we have two stories of resurrection. One is from Judaism, where personal resurrection is not as important as it is for us in the Christian faith. The other is out of our Christian roots, from the Gospel of John. Both are stories that tell us that wherever there is hopelessness, wherever there is despair, wherever there is death, we have a message of life, of new life given to dry bones.

The story from Ezekiel is far more graphic than the stories of the resurrection from the New Testament. This is not a "three days in the grave" story. It is a "many months in the dry sun" story. There is nothing but a valley of dry bones, and it is God who has taken Ezekiel and given him this vision. In this vision we have nothing but "dry bones" and the question, "Can these bones live?" and the great answer of Ezekiel, "O Lord GOD, you know." You know whether or not these "dry bones" will live again. Then we have that beautiful text that inspired the wonderful African-American hymn of how the bones begin to be connected to each other and then they fill with sinews and muscle and are covered with skin and old dry bones are alive again. Nothing that Hollywood has produced could match this story from Ezekiel. It is a wonderful story, that says just when you think that life could be embalmed, life refuses that embalming and comes back.

I believe this is a very important message for those of us who live in the city of Los Angeles this morning. In parts of the city there is nothing but charred skeletons of buildings. The question from our God this morning is, "Can these structures, can these charred bones, can these charred skeletons have life again?" Our answer should be the same as Ezekiel's answer: "O Lord GOD, you know."

Then the word of God will come again to us as it did to Ezekiel: "Call for the breath from the four winds." For the breath and the spirit—which are the same word in the Old Testament and indeed in many languages—the breath, the liveliness, the animus, the élan, must come from the four winds. We cannot seek information and support and advice from only one direction. If those bones in Ezekiel were to live, the breath had to come from the four winds. If the charred remains of South Central and other parts of Los Angeles are to live again, the breath has to breathe from all four directions. All of us, not just African Americans, not just Hispanic Americans, not just the people who live in South Central L.A., but all of us need to be part of the breathing of new life into that area. Ask for the breath from the four winds to come.

I was very pleased when our African-American mayor, Tom Bradley, asked Peter Ueberroth, a surburbanite of German ancestry, from a different direction of the wind, to come over and begin to piece things together in some way. I like even more Ueberroth's answer: "I am not going to do it by myself. We have to have the cooperation of everybody if everything is going to be all right." He mentioned the churches and he mentioned business people, the big people and the little people. Everybody needs to help. I am so pleased that we have received calls from our churches and individuals in the suburban areas saying, "What can we do?" From the four winds the breath is already coming and saying, "We want to breathe new life into the City of Angels." And so there will be new life because the breath is blowing from the four winds. The truth that Ezekiel learned in that vision is the truth that Angelenos can also learn today as we open ourselves to all of the spirit that is blowing from the four winds.

We are not a city of looters, and we are not a city of insensitive people. We do have some looters, and we do have some insensitive people but, above all, we have great human beings as well. On Thursday, about forty pastors from the Los Angeles District of the United Methodist Church gathered at the district superintendent's office and we began working on what we can do, what is it that the church can and should be doing. One of the first things that was shared with us was a FAX from the Council of Bishops of our denomination, which was meeting in Louisville, Kentucky. They immediately felt that they had to make a statement and had to encourage those of us in Los Angeles. They said:

> The Council of Bishops of the United Methodist Church expresses its outrage at the failure of the jury to find any of the defendants guilty in the beating of Rodney King in Los Angeles. The endorsing of police misconduct in this matter is unacceptable. We express our full support of the religious community of Los Angeles in its efforts to seek justice and to curb violent and destructive responses to this verdict. We join with them in prayer for the people of Los Angeles and that justice might prevail in the future.

The wind blew from that direction to Los Angeles, and our own bishop, Jack Tuell, made this personal statement:

> I have a deep sense of outrage and anguish over the results of the trial of the four defendants in the Rodney King beating. This grows out of the message which this verdict seems to send, that the brutal beating of a defenseless man by police is all right. In God's world, that is not all right. I wholeheartedly commend our pastors and leaders, leaders of other religious faiths, and civic leaders, who, though dismayed by this result, are calling for constructive action rather than violence and destruction. Christians can and ought to be indignant over blatant injustice, but our Lord calls us to respond in ways that are loving and nonviolent even to the most hurtful wrongs. I call upon all of our people to join in prayer for all persons involved in the Rodney King incident and trial, for all the families of those who died and for those injured and for all the people of Los Angeles. Let us pray not only that the present violence will cease, but that we may commit

ourselves anew to addressing the economic, social, and political conditions in our society which provide the breeding ground for violence. Until that happens, there will be no true peace in our community.

The United Methodist Committee on Relief, which immediately comes to help communities that have been ravaged or devastated by natural or human violence, has already established an Advanced Special, meaning that all United Methodists throughout the world can now send money through the United Methodist Church to South Central Los Angeles through this medium called "United Methodist Committee on Relief"—UMCOR. The wind is also blowing from New York. From the four winds there is new life coming toward the charred remains of our community and the dry bones will live again.

Our Jewish ancestors gave us the Ezekiel dry bones story, but we also have this wonderful fishing story in the New Testament in the Gospel of John. As all fishing stories go, there are elements of exaggeration in it, and it is a very funny story if you read it carefully and if you just allow your mind to have a little bit of a good time with it even in the midst of tragic moments.

The disciples are disheartened. Their Lord has died. Oh sure, they have already had a couple of apparitions that tell them that he lives, but they are still confused. "What do we do now?" Peter, who is reputed to be the first pope, has this great idea. The first papal bull in history was, "I'm going fishing." Well, what else can you do? Back to the basics. "I'm going fishing" was not "I'm going to have a good time," because fishing, for Peter, was drudgery. It was his job, not fun. For most of us here, fishing means taking a day off, going away, relaxing, but for Peter it meant, "I'm going back to work." A lot of times, in the midst of the most difficult situation, it is in the recovery of our routines that things begin to fall in place. "I'm going to work, I'm going to do what I have always done, and I'm going to do it well."

This is a time when those of us who live in Los Angeles need to recover our routines, need to go back to the basics.

For in the midst of our routines we will discover that there will be answers, as indeed happened to Peter and the disciples. They were in the middle of their routines, and they probably were not going about it very well, or even if they were going about it as well as they could, they still were not able to get a good catch. Then in the midst of all of that, there comes a vision of the Lord appearing to them again and saying, "Fish the other way," and they cast the net and pull in a great catch. There weren't any "this big" that got away. They caught them all, and we are told that they caught 153 fish.

Why 153 fish? What is so magical about the number 153? Was it just a number chosen at random? According to Jerome, that was the total number of fish known at the time. Now I can believe that. I really believe that the author of the Gospel of John intended this story to be a simile, an image, a vision for the church. We all fit in the nets of the church, all 153 of us: Mexicans, Germans, Polish, British, African Americans, Native Americans, non-gay and gay, and everybody else fits in that net.

In this story, the nets do not break. If you look at the parallel stories in Matthew and Luke, which take place during the life of Jesus and not after the resurrection, you will find that the nets were tearing. But not in this one. I believe that what is true for the church is true for the city. All 153 kinds of us will fit, and do fit, in this city. Even if the net is strained to the max right now, it will not break. We will put it together. We will learn to live together in the name of God and for the love of each other.

Isn't it interesting that it was not a religious leader who told us that we could stay together, or who pleaded with us that we stay together, but instead it was Rodney King himself who asked for that? One of the commentators, after King made his statement on Friday, said, "Eloquence comes in many guises." I can tell you, as someone who uses words as part of my trade, that the Rodney King statement—stammering, slow, fishing for words—was one of the most eloquent statements ever made in this city. Listen to how he ended.

"We've gotta quit. We've got to quit. I can understand the first upset in the first two hours after the verdict, but to go on, to keep going on like this and to see a security guard shot on the ground, it's just not right. It's just not right because those people will never go home to their families again and, I mean, please, can we get along here? We all can get along. We've just got to. Just got to. We're all stuck here for a while."

All 153 of us are stuck here for a while. This is our city. I'm not leaving and I don't see anyone else here leaving. We are going to stay here. We are going to repair the city. We are going to rebuild the city. It is not accidental that the ministers of the Los Angeles District decided that what we were going to do between now and the next few months ahead was going to be called "Operation Resurrection." We are the people of the resurrection. We have a great challenge in this city, but we are not going to leave. We are all "stuck here," caught in this net, the net of the church, the net of the City of Angels, the net of a geography that is a gift of God, of a weather that is the envy of most of the world, and of a city that can be and will be a human and humane city "undimmed by human tears" as "America the Beautiful" so wonderfully states.

But, also in "America the Beautiful," we have this prayer: "America, America, God mend thine every flaw." And God, do we have flaws to mend! But we will mend those flaws better if we get more in a repairing, resurrecting kind of a mood rather than in a judging mood. And if we are going to be judgmental at all, then let's make sure that the path of judgment goes back many, many years, perhaps even centuries, to try to understand behavior, lest we think that rioting or looting is the first kind of violence that occurred instead of seeing that there is a preceding violence that has gone on for years to which some of the rioting is a responsive violence.

Then we'll try to mend "our every flaw" and mend our flawed laws as well, because I believe there is something terrible when we have laws that permit certain parts of our city to have more liquor stores than churches and schools.

I think it is a mistake to simply say that because the framers of the Constitution of our country permitted people to have weapons, today we can have civilians better armed than the police. We have to rethink what the right to bear arms is all about. When that was first written, all you could shoot was one shot, pause, reload, and shoot again. Maybe if we only had those kinds of guns, I might still be in favor of ownership of guns. But when we have guns that shoot so many rounds of ammunition per minute, then it seems to me we have to think again about the original intent in the Constitution. I believe that God wants us to "mend our every flaw," including the flaws in our laws.

I believe, however, that the future is bright, that this city was well and aptly named, the City of Angels, that there are more angels than demons in our city, and that the angels and God will prevail.

Rodney King ended by saying, "Let's try to work it out. Let's try to work it out." And I say to that, "Amen and Amen."

*O*ne Circle

K. Samuel Lee

The Rev. K. Samuel Lee is pastor of Los Angeles First Korean United Methodist Church. He is in charge of English-speaking ministries for the congregation.

Y ou've seen it all. It was all over the city, all over the media. Images of burning buildings, parents and children together looting stores, people on streets with guns randomly shooting, photographs captured by the media depicting Los Angeles as a city at war, people gone crazy beating bystanders to death, bands of marines with rifles in their hands patrolling streets, lines of people extending around a city block trying to get their welfare and Social Security checks. I spent sleepless nights.

You've heard gunshots, shouts of the mob, people yelling and crying out as they watched their lifelong accomplishments and investments disappear in smoke. You've heard politicians, clergy persons, and community activists providing words of wisdom as to what the problems were, and how we should be different from now on.

You've probably felt all the emotions I've felt—the shock, anger, frustration, sadness, and powerlessness. I also felt shame and disgust even at myself. So, I cried and cried. In the circles of my associations, both personal and professional, there are persons who suffered the loss of property, business, and, perhaps more importantly, the sense of hope and trust. The lives of some fifty persons have been taken away. Thousands of people suffered and will continue to suffer from their physical and psychological scars. The war is not over. It will not be over until radical changes take place in our lives and in our society.

A number of us were literally confined in our small condominium on Thursday afternoon, our eyes glued on the TV set. My pastor friends, who were scheduled to fly out of Los Angeles at the conclusion of a nation-wide Korean American church gathering on that Thursday afternoon, were kept in this burning city another day. What perfect timing! Cynicism took the backseat as I witnessed what was happening. Watching the development of the riot depicted by TV stations, we were in disbelief.

I watched in horror and fear as blacks, Hispanics, whites, the young and the old, went crazy, became animals on the streets, looting, fighting, burning. I cried. How is that possible? Then, deep down in my heart, I knew they were only a reflection of my own humanity. I would do all I could to deny it! I would do all I could to erase those violent memories and images from my mind! I would do all I could to separate myself from the mobsters and gangsters, those animals on the streets. My education, my cultural sensitivity, and my class status would give me room for denial. But I knew deep down in my heart the violence and hatred that also are alive in me. I know how I can turn into a senseless and unreasonable human being who is caught up in an ego trip, power games, the intellectualizing tendency, even the ability to inflict violent wounds to bystanders.

I cried but kept my eyes wide open to remind myself of the fact that even I can turn into an animal on the street. Tears of disappointment and pity were for myself. Anger was directed inwardly toward myself. I sighed at the picture of myself. I cried and cried because of who I am and for what I stand for in relation to others. Then, I cried because of the larger circles to which I belong. We guard ourselves by constructing a series of concentric circles, the boundaries of separation. By these circles we conveniently deny who we are and who we can become to ourselves and to others.

I came to the church on Saturday morning, when the riot was still on, to find that the name of our church, the word *Korean*, which appears twice in our church sign, had been covered over by pieces of cardboard. In my investigation, I concluded that someone from the Caucasian congregation, with whom we jointly own the church property, covered those words in an attempt to preserve our physical plant. I understand the need to preserve our campus. I am a practical person too. Yet, deep down, I felt anger. I felt I was denied who I am. Hurriedly, I took those cardboard pieces down. Then, I cried. I cried because our circles to which we belong often get destroyed or broken by reasons of convenience or rationalization, because we are not willing to stand by our friends when they suffer. I cried, because I see in myself the same timidity and lack of courage.

When Koreans are attacked, whites exclude themselves, separate themselves, and take on an identity of their own. When Japanese are attacked, Koreans will do all they can to say to themselves, "We belong to the circle of Koreans and not of Japanese!" When blacks are attacked, Koreans separate themselves from the common circle, and throw out derogatory mockings. How often I heard those emotionally charged words, "They deserve it! We are not blacks!" When Jews are attacked, we take on the same circle as the attackers with our own refined justifications and say, "They deserve what they get."

We belong to a circle of common humanity. This we cannot break. We share a common destiny and common struggles. The globe in our days is like a ship that caught fire. One section of the ship is burning, but we say, "Hey, that's on the other side of the ship. I don't have to worry about it." The ship is sinking with our apathy.

The circles to which we belong because of our ethnic or religious associations overlap. Our affirmation of this fundamental fact will provide a common vision of humanity, without having to build the walls that separate ourselves from others.

The media showed an African-American couple, Roger and Victoria, who got married without a tuxedo, a wedding dress, a florist, or a photographer in the midst of the aftermath of the riot. I felt good. It showed me clearly what matters the most in life is not anything material. People who live in West Los Angeles, Culver City, Torrance, and even in Orange County came as volunteers to clean up the burned-down buildings and streets. I cried again. I cried this time, praying for unity and peace in this city. I know clearly that to achieve unity and peace we must change. We must bring about radical changes both in our society and in our individual lives.

We must change our racial attitudes and stereotypes. We must change even our individual lifestyles. So often our lifestyles conveniently create another circle of separation from others, especially from those who live distant from us economically, socially, or culturally. We must change to recognize that when my neighbor is hurting, I, too, hurt. The sinking ship is my own. When we guard ourselves by drawing a series of circles under the disguise of security and protection, we merely separate ourselves and build walls of separation around us. It only produces apathy, insensitivity, and more distance from the rest of society.

We must awaken ourselves. We must awaken from our apathy and insensitivity. We must realize our common struggles and destiny as human beings with a common vision for a better world. We must transform our social policies and political process. We must transform our educational system. All this will begin to take place as we recognize that we belong to the same circle, we share the same vision, we participate in the same struggles.

Multitudes of people are responding to the call to help after the riot. I hope we give generously. Some others are volunteering to help clean up our city streets. I hope we clean up not only our streets, but also ourselves. I hope we clean up our own prejudices, biases, apathies, and insensitivities, even to the point of changing our own lifestyles. In so doing, we'll witness a more fundamental renewal, the rebuilding of the city—not simply the streets of Los Angeles, but also the circle that binds us as one humanity.

*N*o More Business as Usual

David K. Farley

The Rev. David K. Farley is senior pastor of Echo Park United Methodist Church a multi-ethnic congregation in the heart of Los Angeles.

There was a dark cloud over the city of Los Angeles this past week. Flames ignited by a racist verdict and fanned by years of neglect and injustice destroyed the homes, the livelihood, and maybe even the hopes of innocent persons of all races. The city raged. The city cried. The city wounded itself in its anger.

We are angry. For many of us, our anger is mostly focused on the Rodney King verdict and how it represents more than some isolated aberration, but rather a deep, long-term, widespread injustice. For some of us, our anger is focused on those who burn and loot and, out of either anger and frustration or greed and desperation, destroy parts of the city we love. And maybe for most of us the anger is directed at both. But whatever the focus of our anger, we can all join with Jesus as he weeps over the city saying, "would that even today you knew the things that made for peace."

Almost two thousand years ago there was a dark cloud over the city of Jerusalem. There was a crucifixion. Destruction and death seemed to reign. People had hoped that after years of oppression and suffering, after years of hopelessness and despair, their salvation had come. But then there was the verdict: "Crucify him!" The hope was crushed and the world fell apart.

And for many of us, in our personal lives, there is a dark cloud over our hearts. There is anger over our own hurts, there is fear about our own future, there is pain over how others have treated us, there is guilt over how we have treated others. So we, like the disciples following the crucifixion, hide behind shut doors, afraid of the outside world. Or we, like the looters, express our despair in self-destructive ways—hurting ourselves and those close to us.

There are times in our personal lives and in our life as a community when we face the fire—when fear burns inside us, or grief and pain singe our souls; when bitterness and resentment flame up in our hearts, blinding us with its heat and smoke. There are times in our lives when fire would seem so great that we believe our destruction is certain. We can hear no words of love over its crackling. We can see no images of hope beyond its flames. As Bruce Springsteen says:

When the night's quiet and you don't care anymore
And your eyes are tired, and there's someone at
　　your door,
and you realize you wanna let go.
And the weak lies and the cold walls you embrace
eat at your insides and leave you face to face
with streets of fire, streets of fire.

Each of us walk the streets of fire at times in our lives. Whether we come through these times as charred ruins or whether we come through them as refined silver depends on whether or not we have opened ourselves to God's presence with us in those times. If we meet the God of justice and compassion in the fire, then it will refine; if we do not, the fire will destroy.

Our scripture this morning has a powerful message for
those who have come through fire and pain and who seek
to make sense of it.

Last Sunday I spoke about Thomas demanding to
touch the wounds of the crucified one in order to believe in
the resurrected one, and how we must touch the wounds of
the Christ in the suffering of our neighbors if we are to
experience the resurrection. We must not lock ourselves
away in fear. We must be sent forth as Jesus sent forth his
disciples from their hiding place behind the shut doors. We
are sent forth to understand how and why people hurt.

This is the first thing I believe the resurrection gospel
tells us about dealing with this situation. You cannot deal
with it by pretending you can hide from it, or arm yourself
against those threatening forces "out there."

The wounds in our city are deep and unattended: a 50
percent unemployment rate in some of our neighborhoods,
an increasingly widening gap between the rich and the
poor, a siege mentality among many in law enforcement
that tends to view whole communities as "the bad guys."
When vast sections of the population of a city have no stake
in its economy, no access to its decision-making process,
and no sense of being protected or served by its legal
system, then the smoldering has already begun, and all
that is needed is a gust of wind for the inferno to start.

When people are neither protected nor served by the
law, then lawlessness reigns. Lawlessness reigned long
before the explosion of last week, and our neighborhoods
have been looted for years. As Woody Guthrie said in his
song about "Pretty Boy Floyd the Outlaw": "Some rob you
with a six gun; and some with a fountain pen." These are
hard realities to face, but our faith tells us that we cannot
receive the resurrected one unless we receive the crucified
one. We must know and understand our city's wounds if we
as a city are to have new life.

The second way in which the disciples tried to deal with
the trauma of the crucifixion, and that first appearance of the
resurrected one pressuring them to get out from behind the
shut door, was to try to get back to normal, to return to

business as usual. Peter says, "I'm going fishing." The others like the idea. "We will go with you," they say. But this response was not productive. As the scripture says, "They went out, got into the boat; but that night, they caught nothing."

Those who believe in resurrection do not go back to normal following the crucifixion. They go on to new life. And we already see the signs of that new life here in L.A. Like the resurrected Christ cooking breakfast on the shoreline, we have begun our "Operation Resurrection," setting up networks to bring food to the hungry, housing to the homeless, seedling the burned ground with renewed community efforts to bring healing and justice. For us to return to normal would be to return to the tomb. We do not go forth with our brooms and our shovels, like the women went to the tomb, to clean the body. We go forth to prepare the way for new life. No more business as usual.

Finally, another response to all this is to give in to a sense of impotence. "Yes we care, but we are powerless to do anything about it." I believe it is this kind of spirit in Peter that Jesus challenged when he kept asking him, "Do you love me?" "Yes I love you, Jesus, but what can I do?" "Feed my sheep," says Jesus. Do we know and love the resurrected Christ? Well, then we have a hungry world to feed. And we can do it. Christ says go out into the deep and throw out your nets again. "Don't tell me there aren't enough resources. God has provided enough if you are guided by my love."

I am disturbed by some of the news reports about how nothing was done after the Watts riots. It's true that things have gotten worse in many ways. But some of these reports seem to imply that nothing can or will be done. It's almost as if we are being prepared to lower our expectations, as if we are being set up for failure. But we are an Easter people, and we are called to claim the resources and the power to bring God's justice to the city of the angels and to heal its broken heart. Let us come now to the communion table that our hungers might be fed and that we might be nourished and strengthened for the work ahead.

A Call to Be Accountable

James M. Lawson, Jr.

*The Rev. Dr. James Lawson is pastor of Holman
United Methodist Church. He is a nationally known
leader who is active in the Southern Christian
Leadership Conference and other pursuits of
social justice.*

Romans 12:14

Easter is a call to be accountable. Since the 19th of April we have been addressing different angles of the Easter message. Of course on this day, when many of us are still stunned, we are wondering how to appropriate what we have witnessed in this country, in this city. This has been an event unlike any this nation has ever witnessed before. Today, then, I want to raise again an Easter message, "A Call to Be Accountable to God." I chose as a text the 12th verse of the 14th chapter of the book of Romans, where in the word to the church in Rome, Paul writes, "So then, each of us will be accountable to God." It can be translated also, "So, then, each of us will be answerable to God alone." Or as other scholars have lifted it up—"to God alone we will be answerable."

Now, for most of us gathered here in this sanctuary this morning, we assume, and even take for granted, the notion that, yes indeed, there is a moral garment across the universe that we call God, and that we are judged by that moral garment. Yes, we must be accountable to God! Yes! We reap what we sow! God is never mocked for or by the human race.

And yet, it is strange how, when the kinds of circumstances we've seen occur over the last three or four days, there is a sort of notion, "Well that's true, but it is only true for those who are directly involved in the business. Only those who burned will be accountable to God. Only those who have looted. But the rest of us are not." Our President reminded us last night, "let nobody go about talking about something being wrong with America." These statements lead us to believe that there is no accountability that moves across our society. If we want to know, as so many reporters are asking so many different people—and I have declined to answer many calls from reporters across the last several days—if they want to know who is responsible, and if we want to know, then let us ask ourselves, "Why is America destroying, killing people in Central America? Why are American tax dollars ravaging Mozambique and Angola? Why are we Americans killing each other at such a high rate? Why is there so much rape and family abuse and wife battering and all of the rest of the violence that goes on in our society?

If we try to understand all that is happening among us, then we will understand the urban explosion in Los Angeles. Then we will recognize that indeed we had better learn to say that our nation is accountable to God. Already, as Malcolm X said some years ago, "the chickens are coming home to roost everyday." But because some of us are isolated and insulated, because some of us eat three square meals a day, because some of us live in the right places, we think we are not aware of the way in which so many other of our fellow citizens, especially women and children in Los Angeles today, are the primary victims of what is going on.

Easter is a call to be accountable. We are accountable to God in the way in which we grow as persons before God. No matter what the human situation is, every man and every woman has an accountability to the image of God that has been planted in them. There is a responsibility that we each have to make certain that we continue exploring the deep spiritual journey, the journey inward and outward.

Who here would pretend that we have reached the full height of the maturity that we have found in the face of God in Jesus of Nazareth? Who here would pretend that we have arrived in fulfilling in our own lives the promises of God, indeed that we belong to God, that God is ours? If we search ourselves, and if we search ourselves on behalf of our nation, we know full well that the longing of our hearts has not yet been fulfilled. Deep dreams that we all have for ourselves and for our world are not yet norms by which we think and live and move and have our being and strength. We are accountable to God. We are accountable to God in the sense that each of us and all of us are called to join God's human family.

We like, in our times, to talk about a lack of self-worth, a lack of self-esteem, the lack of a sense, on the inside, of meaning. Cornell West of Princeton University has pointed out in recent months the nihilism that is so much a part of the American scene. That nihilism is so much a part even of the African-American scene. Many not only do not have a sense that they are a child of God, but many, in fact, hate themselves. Whose responsibility is this nihilism? It is the responsibility of all of America.

Early this morning as Dorothy and I were dressing, we had one of the news stations on. We could not help but recall the numbers of reports that kept coming through of the Korean-American businesses that had been burned. But no word did we hear, for the better part of an hour, no word in all that we heard, of the black American businesses that had been burned and looted. But this is of course one of the things that is happening in Los Angeles. Perhaps that is the way of the whole future, of the disconnectedness that people feel even in the black community, the disconnectedness that so many Americans feel who do not think they belong to the human race.

There have been many episodes among some of us who have been out in the streets, while stopping a looter or walking and seeing it, and saying to someone, "Well, why are you doing this? Don't you know that this is our community?" "We don't care!" has often been the response. "We don't have any relationship to this." What a sad state of affairs! But I insist that they haven't learned this from the churches or the synagogues. They have learned this from the society. They have learned this from the way in which we, as a people, will not organize for the things that need to be accomplished in our midst. So then each of us will be accountable to God.

Are we, then, accountable enough to join the human family? In the episode from the Gospel of John (John 21:1–19), this accountability is a part of the word that Jesus is trying to get across to his people. (The episode describes the presence of male disciples, but I am more than persuaded that there is no doubt that men and women were gathered at that site in Galilee.) Jesus confronts Peter, "Do you love me?" Peter, from the very beginning, I suppose, doesn't understand why he is being asked these questions by his friend. "Of course I love you." Jesus responds, "Feed my lambs!" The second time, "Tend my sheep!" The third time, "Feed my sheep!" The fourth time, Jesus said, "Follow me!" That is, "if you love me, Peter, our friendship is solid. You see me as the Messiah. You hear me as the one who has brought into your life in a fresh fashion the very presence of God. All of that is well and good. But, if your relationship with me is a relationship of harmony and joy and power and truth, then do something about it in the world. Follow me. Feed my sheep. Deal with the human race that needs healing and lifting."

If there is a mood in the church that needs to be challenged, it is a mood that when a catastrophe such as this comes through a community—whether it be Westwood, Melrose, downtown, Compton, Long Beach, South Central, Crenshaw, West Adams, USC, East Los Angeles, or Koreatown—when such a catastrophe comes, none of us are apart from it. All of us must not join the looting or the burning or the bashing of other people. But all of us must join the issues. "Follow me." Get into the business of working the works of God so that indeed the social alienation that continues to rise and the pain of so many people can be seen and heard and counted as real.

There is a little book out that I have seen but have not read yet. I have seen as least two book reviews of it, though, and I intend to buy it when I return from General Conference. It is entitled, *The Harrowing of Mozambique*. In one of the reviews, I saw the author's remark concerning the district commissioner responsible for the care of over two hundred thousand refugees who have been dislodged from Mozambique, a country whose agony of which we must repent. This author says something like this: When asked why he is so concerned and why he is spending his life for those two hundred thousand refugees from across the border, the district commissioner said, "We think we can be uninvolved. But, we are involved. That naked man there," he said, "he is you. He is me. Mankind (those are his words), mankind did this." But humankind can also change it.

I am grateful to God that so many of you have not gone off in the wrong direction as we have been appalled and dismayed. But, rather, you have come to Holman to help serve in different ways—bringing food, giving money, and organizing creatively. Serving our city in order that we can be engaged in healing the wounds, feeding the hungry, lifting up the needs of the people—and, I will add, continuing to work for justice. We will also continue to work that the police department be reformed. We will also continue to work that the criminal justice system will be changed so that the poor and the young and the people of color can gain justice in our midst.

If we are so engaged, then indeed, we have heard the Easter call, a call to be accountable to God, the God Almighty. Amen.

Songs, Shepherds, and Social Earthquakes

Peggy Owen Clark

The Rev. Peggy Owen Clark is senior pastor of Hollywood-Beverly Christian Church, Los Angeles. These are her reflections in looking back on the Sunday after the rioting.

It was the Sunday after the Los Angeles riots, and the congregation gathered for Bible study before worship. I was worried that some of the folks would not show up as the fires had been perilously close on Hollywood Boulevard and the looting had come up to within a block of the church. The days and nights had been tense and long preceding our gathering, and yet the spirit among the people was animated.

Sharing of the feelings of despair, confusion, anger, and sorrow all burst forth as we tried to make sense out of an incredible drama. The plates had shifted. Like the geographic plates that shift under California fault lines when pressure becomes too intense and causes an earthquake, the social plates of frustration that had been building for some twenty-seven years had caused a natural disaster. Like an earthquake, its damage was selective. But unlike most earthquakes, this one had plenty of warning.

I had planned for the Creative Worship Sunday bulletin at Hollywood-Beverly Christian Church, a program of Great Hymns of the Church. As the worship service began and we approached the time of hymn singing, I had felt vaguely guilty about singing songs in a crisis. And yet it occurred to me that there is no better time to sing a hymn than in the face of fear. Some sang with hesitant spirits. Some sang bravely to summon courage. We recalled the Disciples singing in the most trying situations, as if to bolster our faith.

But the Sunday after the riots, the whole story of the days of fire and fury was just about to be told. It was a tale of corporate shame, of racial intolerance, of law enforcers fearful of the very people they were to protect, and government leaders who were swift to point fingers and lay blame.

Those of us who were citizens of this great city, whether longtime residents or recent arrivals, began to try to put together the pieces and reexamine a lot of assumptions. For people of faith it was a difficult task. We who huddled together to sing hymns wondered if things would ever become routine. The next Sunday was Mother's Day. The day usually reserved for sentimentality and familial devotion had been eclipsed by a recovering people. The lectionary reading was the Twenty-third Psalm, and somehow it seemed most appropriate for a disoriented flock to think about shepherding and nurture.

In the midst of a crisis, where foodstuffs and baby food and gasoline and water were in short supply, we heard the words: "The Lord is my shepherd, I shall not want."

The words resonated with the spirit of all of us who at that moment felt like a motherless or fatherless child. Most of the struggle of parenting has to do with providing food, clothing, education, shelter, and security in this very difficult time. Who would provide? Who would be the shepherd to a city torn apart? Who would look after the wants of a divided community?

We recited the words that followed: "He restores my soul." Was there anything more of a challenge to us on that morning than restoring the soul of a city? I do not believe that the problems of the Los Angeles riots will ever be solved merely by philanthropy. The hard task, after the generosity and funding have faded, will be to do "soul work," the task of restoring a sense of balance, integrity, purpose, and love to our common life and work.

Part of "restoring our souls" means that the religious community in Southern California will be called to be less peripheral to the lives of many and to be teachers of foundational truths to live by. Part of our tasks as shepherds (clergy and laity alike) to the culture is that we must restore value and meaning to our common existence. We listened to the next words: "He leads me in right paths for his name's sake." This is where the message hit home for all of us. Our corporate indifference to the suffering of the poor has allowed us not to be leaders, prophetic pathfinders in God's name. Perhaps it has not occurred to us that to lead people in right living was as much a part of the Great Commission as was baptizing and witnessing. What does the psalmist say after this passage? "I fear no evil; for you are with me." This could mean that forging ahead in righteousness means freedom from fear. It could mean that evil will never be triumphant where people feel secure in the faith. The church had become for many the one institution in the riots that told the truth, remained the same, did not lay blame, and got to work. (The immediate response and visible presence of the churches may have been stronger than a thousand sermons preached that day).

"Your rod and your staff—they comfort me." We have all recited these words over and over. Have we ever stopped to think what was meant by the rod, what the staff represented? The entire psalm is poetic, and this part was not meant to be literal. I believe the psalmist is referring to the *rod of discipline* and the *staff of compassion*. They are inextricably intertwined, for compassion needs the ability to say no, and discipline needs to be tempered with love. Perhaps what the psalmist is saying to us is that through discipline and compassion we can establish the kind of leadership that forges new paths in righteousness and restores the souls of the brokenhearted.

Pierre Wolff, in his book, *May I Hate God?* says:

> Hatred is present as long as people are mute, but as soon as they decide to express the anger that is in their heart...something is already changing and maybe is already changed.[1]

The Lord's Prayer was never more needed than in a troubled time when people speak with dishonest hearts. If we were as honest as we should be, we would not have permitted racial intolerance to exist under the guise of cultural diversity. If we were as honest as we should be, we would not have permitted the words *law and order* to be code words for brutality and repression. If we were as honest as we should be, we would have realized that God shepherds through our words and deeds, and the rod and the staff are ours to claim.

Social earthquakes do not happen because of isolated instances any more than geographical earthquakes happen because of one shift or crack. They happen because of a gradual weakening of the plates. The social plates in Los Angeles have survived almost three decades of weakening. Much will be written about the riots, and everyone will have at least ten ideas about what should have been done. But what I found remarkable in the crisis was that the faithful still have voices to sing songs, and that the Word of the Lord still opens to us a message of hope. The restoring of souls is a lifelong task, and one that will require renewed energy from all of us in Southern California. But on those first Sundays in May, it was good to know that shepherds still existed and the church could still sing.

[1]Pierre Wolff, *May I Hate God?* Paulist Press, 1979, p. 59.

Address to the Korean Community

Havanpola Ratanassra

Dr. Havanpola Ratanassra is president of the American Buddhist Congress and Buddhist Sangha Council of Southern California. This address was delivered at Kwan Um Sa Temple, a Korean Buddhist temple on Third St., Los Angeles.

My Dear Friends in the Dharma:

From my office, located in Koreatown, I watched the most deplorable series of events that has ever happened to Los Angeles unfold before my eyes. I watched my neighbors, shopkeepers, and friends be assaulted and their businesses torched. I watched looters run over my lawn and heard gunfire of merchants around the corner, desperately protecting their shops.

Kwan Um Sa Temple has been a major part of the Buddhist Sangha Council of Southern California. I want you to know, therefore, that the Sangha Council stands completely behind the Korean community. We look out for your interests, as well as the interests of other Asians and all Buddhists. And in the midst of the shock, anger, and sorrow that has followed last week, I have an urgent message to convey to you:

It is not enough to simply say I am deeply concerned with the disturbances that have occurred. It is not enough to offer sympathy to the victims, the civilians who were hurt, and the merchants who lost everything they worked hard for. It is not enough to say "this should never have happened in this civilized city of Los Angeles." It *has* happened. And we are more than simply "concerned." We are much, much more than concerned. We are taking direct action. In fact, we had already started before all this broke out. It is ironic to think that, just a few weeks before the violence started, our colleagues in the InterReligious Council—the leaders of other religious traditions—all agreed to start concrete programs that would really deal with the problems of escalating violence in our city.

We have started late. And yet, perhaps more good can come of this. We now have the attention of the nation and our politicians, whereas we might not have been able to get it before. We have the deep interest and offer of direct assistance from the corporate business community, who before had no interest in the inner city. Everywhere, people of all ethnic backgrounds are talking seriously about dealing with the root of the problem.

It may be tiresome to hear, but now is *not* the time for anger or hatred. While we still hold the spotlight, now is the time for action and solidarity. Let us seize the moment to work out problems between our ethnic and religious groups. Let us rebuild our city *properly*, to be a place of prosperity, where our children can grow up in a true multi-ethnic community, a community based on understanding, tolerance, and peace. This is the Buddhist way. Other groups are ready and willing. The InterReligious Council is forming special committees to propose both immediate and long-term changes that will greatly benefit everyone: Asians, Latinos, blacks, and whites. The Koreans must be on those committees. I urge you to join us. Together, we will force the issue of positive change.

After the Simi Valley Verdict:

A *Christian Confession of* Conscience

The Los Angeles Theological Reflection
Group, May 15, 1992

"Riot is the language of the unheard."
Martin Luther King, Jr.

The stunning April 29 acquittal of four white police
officers charged with assaulting black motorist Rodney
King took Los Angeles literally by storm. In its wake
this storm left fifty-eight people dead, more than five
thousand buildings torched, and a city in a state of shock.
Now it is encumbent upon those of us who reside here to
make sense of these dramatic events.

We are a group of concerned Christians, lay and clergy,
who have devoted ourselves to the work of justice, peace-
making, and service in this city. We are part of a group that
has met regularly for several years to reflect theologically
and politically on our work. Many of us are, like the Simi
Valley jury, persons who by race and class inheritance
belong to the dominant culture. We feel compelled to make

this public statement because those in this city with race and class privilege are avoiding taking responsibility for the violence and disruption.

Therefore we make this confession: *The Simi Valley verdict revealed the truth*—not the truth about what happened to Rodney King, but the truth about the dominant culture. Sadly, history has yet again demonstrated that the dominant culture remains blind to race and class oppression and deaf to the cries of the disenfranchised *unless and until* there is a riot. As people committed to nonviolent social transformation we cannot endorse the recent violence; indeed we feel profoundly saddened by it, particularly the loss of life and jobs and hope. But we must recognize that we too bear responsibility for it. Indeed, *as long as violence remains the language by which the dominant culture maintains its power, the unheard will be forced to use violence to reach us with their demands for justice.*

The rebellion we have just witnessed compels us to acknowledge the judgment of the gospel in this historical moment. In light of it we seek to repent (literally, to "change directions"). In our tradition this also requires that we make judgments of our own about some issues that arise out of the immediate aftermath of the rebellion.

I. Why did this happen?

> Some of the Pharisees in the crowd said to him, "Teacher, order your disciples to stop." He answered, "I tell you, if these were silent, the stones would shout out."
>
> Luke 19:39-40

Anticipating the possibility of an unjust verdict in the LAPD officers' trial, religious and civic leaders urged residents to remain calm, admonishing protesters to vent their anger in socially acceptable ways. It was not to be: with every fire set and every stone hurled, the silenced anguish of the marginalized cried out.

In the aftermath we continue to hear a double refrain from the politicians, media commentators, and other moralists. They lament the verdict but condemn the riots: "Nothing justifies such behavior," they scold. But why wasn't the daily cycle of violence experienced by the poor of our city enough to command their attention? Had there been a verdict and no riot, would the Mayor, the Governor, and the President have rushed to the scene? Would they be huddling with their advisors on urban problems and policy? On the other hand, we hear clarion calls for healing and pious promises to "rebuild our community." But does this chorus yet understand the wounds? Will we once again sow the seeds of destruction in the reconstruction?

Our churches are particularly culpable. *"If my disciples remain silent*, the stones will cry out." Why have we Christians learned to live with the injustices that became intolerable for those who rebelled? Why do we too remain silent about the daily violence that the poor must live with, and speak out only when property is burned and looted and *white* lives are lost? And does not our endorsement of the militarization of our city suggest that we are captive to the values of the dominant culture, that we too will go to great lengths to protect privilege rather than stand in solidarity with the poor?

We Christians need to repent of our silence. This means intensifying our efforts to identify and address the roots of injustice in our city. It means *opening up* the conversation about the problems, not shutting it down through heavy-handed law and order. The liturgical season of Pentecost is the time when the church remembers its vocation to carry on the work of Jesus in the power of the Spirit. **We therefore call on our parishes and our denominational leaders to devote the entire season of Pentecost to sober reflection upon the meaning of these riots, in order to deepen our comprehension of their rootedness in structural injustice.**

- In the meantime, we believe the sum total of violence in our city must be reduced. We understand that many in our communities welcomed the deployment of the National Guard and federal troops and agents in L.A. We believe however that this massive military response came too late to stop the violence. Their continued presence is serving only a political function and threatens to perpetuate the cycle of domination in which the poor are caught. We also believe that our reliance on federal troops reveals our lack of moral imagination. **We call on the churches to support long-term efforts to promote community policing strategies.**

• The lessons we draw from the recent violence are diametrically opposed to those of the National Rifle Association in its cynical campaign to lift what little restraint remains upon the marketing of firearms. The problem isn't that there aren't enough guns to guarantee public safety, but that there are far too many. Our children have learned from our leaders about being armed; who will show them how to disarm? **We urge state and federal legislators to enact and enforce strict gun control laws**.

• The issue of police abuse must not be lost in the riot-related turmoil. **We join other groups in insisting that Chief Daryl Gates step down immediately so that Chief-designate Willie Williams can begin the difficult challenge of rebuilding community trust. We urge a timely and vigorous federal investigation into civil rights violations by the four LAPD officers, and their dismissal from the force. We also support the Police Accountability Act (H.R. 2972) now being considered by Congress.**

II. Who is responsible?

Or those eighteen who were killed when the tower of Siloam fell on them—do you think that they were worse offenders than all the others living in

Jerusalem? No, I tell you; but unless you repent, you will all perish just as they did.

Luke 13:4-5

Many, particularly politicians and the press, are trying to avoid responsibility for the riots by perpetuating a discourse that divides city residents into "bad people" (looters and "hoodlums") and "good people" (clean-up brigades and "law-abiding citizens"). Such false distinctions only mask the complicity of *all* who live in the city.

How can those in unaffected neighborhoods lament that "they are only hurting themselves," when the message of arson is precisely that people feel disowned in their own city? How can we call the looters "hooligans" when they have learned to "take what you can when you can" from white collar criminals, such as those involved in the Savings and Loan scandal? When executives of our major corporations increase their salaries while exporting jobs to the Third World and laying off workers at home, who is looting whom? How can we call those using fire or guns "thugs" when they have learned from U.S. foreign policy to prosecute grievances with violence? "Violence must *always* be condemned," said President Bush while in L.A.; was he including Panama and Iraq? The actions of the disenfranchised in our society only mirror the moral climate modeled by those in power.

Another avoidance is race-scapegoating. The images captured make it clear that this was a truly "multicultural riot." Race is not the issue; but *racism is*. The dominant culture is deliberately playing on racial tensions in order to obscure the deeper issues of class disparity (e.g. the way in which the media played upon already extant tensions between African Americans and Korean Americans in its coverage of the riot). The looters were from *all* ethnic backgrounds—but most were poor. The welfare system, contrary to Reagan-Bush apologists, is not the issue; *long-smoldering resentment at institutionalized economic inequity is*.

We Christians need to repent of the compulsion to blame others. We must instead take our share of responsibility for a system that is simply not working for a large sector of our population. Only then we can resist the logic of those now clamoring to make examples of rioters. We believe that extraordinary security measures, as well as vindictive punishment of the some seventeen thousand arrested during the rebellion, only serve to entrench the causes of the riot in the first place: official brutality and the absence of equal justice under the law. **If our churches truly desire healing in our city we must work for reconciliation, not criminalization and revictimization of those driven by racial and economic injustices to riot.**

- Our communities are angry over issues of police accountability, and need to express this publically and politically. To be prevented from peacefully demonstrating only our feelings that authority is being abused. **Therefore we call for an immediate end to the state of emergency and its suspension of basic civil rights**.

- It is unconscionable that the same judicial system that could not convict four white policemen of beating King is now pressing for maximum sentences for looters. **We therefore urge that amnesty be offered to those charged with nonviolent crimes.**

- We are incensed at the duplicity of federal Immigration and Naturalization agents who, though deployed to help keep the peace, instead conducted deportation sweeps, even among people not arrested or charged with crimes. LAPD-INS law enforcement cooperation both contravenes the city's policies and increases the immigrant community's mistrust of the police. **We call for an immediate end to such collaboration, and the release of all undocumented persons not charged with crimes who were caught up in these sweeps.**

III. What should be done?

> As he came near and saw the city, he wept over it,
> saying, "If you, even you, had only recognized on
> this day the things that make for peace! But now
> they are hidden from your eyes....Not leave within
> you one stone upon another; because you did not
> recognize the time of your visitation from God.
>
> Luke 19:41f, 44

Many of us joined in the volunteer initiatives to help
clean up after the rebellion, to distribute food and clothing
to the hardest-hit areas, and to raise money for rebuilding.
Important as these efforts are, we acknowledge that they
are not by themselves enough to loosen the yoke of oppression under which the poor of our city labor. We understand
that transformation cannot occur unless the poor themselves are empowered as social subjects, not objects of
charity.

*We Christians need to repent of our failure "to
recognize the time of visitation."* We must better understand how discriminations based upon race and class
are mutually reinforcing in our society and our churches.
Our churches must vigorously embrace the biblical man-
date to bridge the yawning chasm between the haves and
have-nots (Isaiah 58). Above all, if we are to help insure
that a genuinely new social order is constructed from the
ashes of this uprising, we must listen to, and forge a
practical partnership with, the poor. **We call on the
churches to think creatively how we can produce
jobs and contribute to grassroots development in
our own work. We must also participate in and
critically monitor official efforts to rebuild the ef-
fected communities.**

- The Ueberroth Commission must focus on human
  resources and not just businesses and infrastructure. The people of South Central have long
  struggled to be heard by the Community Redevel-
  opment Agency; downtown forces must not be

allowed to use this situation as a pretext for large capital projects that primarily benefit outside corporate interests. Instead resources should concentrate on job training programs, health and child care centers, and youth recreation facilities. **We call for all decisions concerning major reconstruction efforts to be subject to input and direction from residents of the affected areas.**

• The new order can only be designed and built by residents who will have control over reconstruction resources. **We urge that as reconstruction contracts are awarded, primary consideration should be given to contractors and firms owned and operated by people of color; and local residents, especially unemployed at-risk youth, should be hired to carry out the work.**

Together, with the leaders of our churches and all people of faith, we seek to discover the crucial role we might play in the rebellion's wake. Instead of scolding others, let us see how the seeds of injustice lie within us and the dominant culture from which we benefit. We are disheartened by the violence that has overtaken our city; but we know that because we were silent, the stones cried out in anger against an unjust system. May we come to truly "know the things that make for peace," and give flesh to them in our life and work.

Drafters:

Rev. Thomas Smolich, S.J., Sandy Perluss-Lejeune, *Proyecto Pastoral*

Rev. Gregory Boyle, S.J., Leonardo Vilchis, *Dolores Mission*

Freddie Schrider, *Episcopal Diocese Peace & Justice Commission*

Kieran Prather, Sandra Huckaby, *LA Catholic Worker*

Rev. Jim Schrider, *Christic Institute*

Rev. Luis Olivares, *CMF*
Mary Brent Wehrli, *So. Calif. Interfaith Task Force on Central America*
Rev. Don Kribs, *St. Camillus Center for Pastoral Care*
Ched Myers, *American Friends Service Committee*
Rev. Jane Turner, *St John's Episcopal Church*
Brian Sellers-Peterson, *Bread for the World*
Rev. Chris Ponnet, *Our Lady of Assumption*

(This statement does not reflect the views of the organizations listed; affiliations for identification purposes only.)

For more information, contact Sandy Perluss-Lejeune at Proyecto Pastoral (213) 268-9880.

Captured by God's Vision

Joan Brown Campbell

The Rev. Joan Brown Campbell is general secretary of the National Council of the Churches of Christ in the U.S.A. This address was delivered at the National Workshop on Christian Unity on May 6, 1992 in Denver, Colorado

I have been to Beirut, to Baghdad, Crossroads, Calcutta, and to Nicaragua, to Cuba, to Cambodia. I have stood amidst rubble. I have cried with the people as they buried their dead in Mathari Valley, Kenya and in South Africa. I have witnessed social disintegration, war, and ethnic tension. All of these I have seen in the context of ecumenical team visits designed to witness to Christian solidarity. In every case I have returned to the U.S. to join with others in a response to the human needs witnessed and to work to address the policies of our nation that affect life for those we visited. We have responded with money and food and medicine, and we have even been successful in affecting U.S. policy vis-à-vis South Africa and the Middle East. The truth is that in the last twelve years we

111

have been more effective and diligent in our response to our overseas partners than we have been here in the U.S.A.

Now we come fresh from an ecumenical team visit to Los Angeles. There we stood amidst the rubble, watched a Korean family bury their dead, witnessed social disintegration and ethnic tensions and poverty. No doubt we will be successful in our disaster appeal and I pray that we are, but Los Angeles is a word to the nation, and only the foolish will fail to listen to what is being said.

Come, let me try to give you a mind tour. We saw destruction—random, senseless and widespread. We saw grocery stores burned, along with clinics, cleaners, storefront churches, fast-food stores, banks, whole shopping plazas. No one was immune. Several of the over five thousand fires set in the two days were still smoldering.

We talked to people walking in the streets, working to clean up and rebuild their neighborhood. Some cried because they had nowhere to buy food, diapers, milk for the babies, and because the burning of small neighborhood businesses had taken their jobs. Everywhere there was anger, confusion, and despair. They were angry at the police and fire fighters who failed to protect them, at the gangs who continually terrorize their neighborhood, at the drug pushers who tempt and corrupt their youth, at each other, and at the government.

We saw a massive military presence. It was a bit disquieting to come into the Los Angeles airport and see soldiers with drawn bayonets. It is more than a little uncomfortable to see soldiers on the roofs of the buildings with M-16s loaded and ready to shoot. It is not a comfortable thing to see tanks in the streets filled with armed soldiers. We're more used to seeing that in Baghdad, in Beirut, than we are in Los Angeles. We saw people on the street selling instantly-made Rodney King T-shirts. We saw children and we saw their parents very worried about whether they would be playing in glass, and whether they would be hurt by the now destabilized buildings that might fall at any moment. All throughout that city we saw evidences of unattended-to race issues—Hispanics not at ease with Koreans and blacks, blacks angry with Koreans, Koreans confused by what was happening to them, and Native people hardly even mentioned—and too many whites were doing business as usual.

Are there signs of hope in that city? Yes, there are. I was met at the airport—I was expecting to be met by one of the local pastors. Instead a large yellow taxi drove up and someone said, "Rev. Campbell, we're here to meet you." And I said, "I thought we were being met by the Rev. Chip Murray of the First AME Church." And they said, "Our company has donated our entire fleet of taxis to First AME Church since they are doing such an incredible job of trying to take care of people's needs." They also said that for $1 they now take people from the neighborhoods where there are no grocery stores to where they can shop—the hunger problem is created by the fact that there are no grocery stores where the people can shop—so for $1 this very large taxi company will now take people from their neighborhood to grocery stores outside their neighborhood.

There is hope at First AME Church and if there are any AMEs in the room, they ought to stand tall and proud. What is happening in that congregation is incredible. It is like the epicenter. There, hundreds and hundreds of volunteers are sorting food and clothes and passing it out to a network of at least forty congregations, growing every day. One of the signs of hope, and one of the stories of despair, was that at First AME Church, on the first night of the disturbance, a house very close to the First AME Church was burning. The fire department would not come unless the church would promise protection for the fire fighters, so the men of the church gathered around, shoulder to shoulder, and completely surrounded the fire fighters so they could have the protection they needed from those who were looting and rioting, in order to save that family home.

This is just one of hundreds of stories that could be told. We spent the evening in a Korean church, and I want to tell you the story because it made me perhaps more hopeful for the possibilities for our ecumenical work than anything that's happened to me since I became general secretary. I think you know a little, if not quite a bit, about the tensions between the Korean community and the black community. At my advanced age I have given up thinking things are an accident. I have decided they are indeed providential. It is at this point in our life in the National Council that we have the first Korean president the National Council has ever had. And so it was Syngman Rhee who went with us to the Korean church, but we did not go alone to that church. We asked twelve of the local black clergy if they would go with us to that congregation of six thousand people that was meeting for their regular Wednesday evening prayer meeting—except nothing is regular in Los Angeles right now, because it was also the day of the funeral for an eighteen-year-old young man, a member of that congregation, who had been shot. The possibilities that exist because the churches in the African-American community and the Korean churches may find a way to talk to each other is one of the very hopeful signs, and needed agendas, for the future there in Los Angeles. That these coexist side by side in the NCCC is providential.

Money is pouring into Los Angeles, and I had to say to myself, "It is indeed strange that when we have dire tragedies we respond with generosity and with speed. But when we know they are coming, somehow we cannot muster up the same kind of response and compassion."

Let me share what we said to the people of Los Angeles. There were fifteen of us in the NCCC delegation:

> *The National Council of Churches* comes today to Los Angeles because people are hurting and in need and as people of faith we can do no less. We come to acknowledge that this nation has just experienced the first major tremor in what could be a national social earthquake.
>
> We come because we were asked to be here by our sisters and brothers in the African-American churches and the Korean Presbyterian churches. These churches are active members of the NCCC.

We come to bring both spiritual and material support—an evidence of solidarity from all of the thirty-two member churches.

We come as a Council that is multiracial and multicultural in our membership. We come to offer ourselves in the long-term task of reconciliation and to assist in the urgent and delicate work of helping African-American and Korean communities to reduce tensions and build understanding. The fact that these churches exist side by side in the National Council is a sign of hope and a foundation for increased cooperation.

We come to confess that the sin of racism continues to dominate our nation's life and deny dignity and justice to all people of color. The National Council has long worked for the elimination of all forms of racism and for the development of a compassionate society. In late April the Prophetic Justice Unit of the National Council called the churches to a renewed commitment to racial justice. Even before Los Angeles, it was clear to all who could see that cities were and still are a mass of smoldering embers. Entrenched racism in all of its forms generates cycles of violence, division, and a shattered community.

We come as believers, and we cannot escape the ancient biblical word that if a society fails to care for the poor, the widows, the children, and the stranger at the gate, then it will come under God's judgment.

Yes, we have seen haplessness take brutal form in the streets of Los Angeles, but we must ask, does this not come when a society does not govern itself guided by an inner conviction that each person is of equal value? Economic inequities are ample evidence that liberty and justice for all is more national rhetoric than national reality.

We come to say here in Los Angeles that we in the NCCC will call people of goodwill to:

—REPENTANCE for our refusal to respond to the cries for help;

—REPAIR THE BREACH in our social contracts, to address the sin of racism and poverty that continues to divide us;

—REBUILD THE CITIES upon the solid ground of justice, to rebuild our brokenness and restore our souls;

Then, only then, can we restore order and engage in the larger task of learning to live together.

We begin with a modest offering from our disaster relief office—funds and trained community organizers, but recognizing that social disorder has profound governance and political roots, we wish to use our influence, (and here I would say to every one of you this is my message to this gathered group: *we can* use our influence) as ecumenical and church leaders to create a moral climate and a political will to urge our government, our president, all candidates for office, to commit to a Marshall Plan for our cities focused on quality education, available health care, adequate housing, and jobs that with dignity put food on every table.

I think we cannot afford to be polite. We have to say, "Mr. President, no! Social programs were not the cause of the disturbances in Los Angeles. It is neither right nor fair to trivialize human suffering and to ignore the very real promises that there were in those programs. They were not perfect, but they did not all fail."

The *New York Times* had a marvelous editorial the other day, and just two facts tell you what this is about: spending on direct aid for cities has fallen 60 percent after adjustments for inflation since 1981; the federal share of city budgets fell from 18 percent in 1980 to 6.4 percent in 1990, just as AIDS and crack sent social spending through the roof.

We do not dare to blame the poor. We must find compassionate solutions. If we take seriously the needs of people, then the crises created by the policies of the last twelve years need to be reversed. Then, I think, we can talk about creating order. You know, the Bible speaks about creating new people, new cities, new realities. It does not talk about creating new orders.

Now let's try to put it in a biblical context because that is who we are and that is what instructs us and informs us. The scriptures tell us several times that Jesus wept. In Luke 19:41 the scriptures tell us that Jesus came into Jerusalem, and as he came near he saw the city and he wept over it. The words are so powerful for our day—and Jesus said. "If you, even you, had only recognized on this day the things that make for peace! But now they are hidden from your eyes."

If we listen carefully this very day, I believe we can hear Jesus weeping—weeping for us and for this nation and for the people of Los Angeles, this nation conceived in liberty, this people, who in pledging allegiance to the flag speak the lofty words, "One nation under God, indivisible, with liberty and justice for all."

Jesus weeps for us and for our broken promises and for our dreams deferred. And Jesus says to us, even as he did to the people of Jerusalem, if you, with your dreams of liberty and life and happiness and equality and justice—if you had only recognized those things that make for peace, but now they are hidden from your eyes.

And we ask, how do we open the eyes of the blind, how do we heal the wounds of the nation, how indeed do we form a more perfect union? And God says to us from the ages, "Fall on your knees, turn to me and be healed." Perhaps God is not only weeping with sorrow, but perhaps God is angry with us. For we have failed to behave as the one people we were called to be, and the evidence of our disunity is everywhere. And God must say, "How can the people believe that I am God when even my church is marked by division and by racial isolation?"

But always in the midst of turmoil and despair, God has called forth a leader, a prophet to speak God's word to the nation. And so it was with Isaiah, and possibly there is a lesson for us in the ancient story of the call of Isaiah. It's in the 6th chapter of Isaiah. It begins with that marvelous vision: "In the year that King Uzziah died I saw the Lord sitting on a throne, high and lofty and the hem of this robe filled the temple....' Holy, holy, holy is the LORD of hosts; the whole earth is full of God's glory.'" And then Isaiah says, "Woe is me!... I live among a people of unclean lips; yet my eyes have seen the King, the LORD of hosts!"

What a magnificent vision—anyone with an ounce of imagination or with a little theater in their blood cannot help but be touched by this scripture lesson. In the black church they would say, that text will *preach*—virtually by itself! But let us look at what is happening there. There are four steps. First, Isaiah had a vision and in that vision he saw God in all of God's glory. He didn't initially have a vision of a Great Society. He had a vision of God—Holy, Holy, Holy. He is filled with the wonder and majesty of it all, and in the light of the vision of power and love and beauty and grace he recognizes his own unworthiness. And that is the second step: he confesses his inadequacies, his sinfulness, but he confesses them in the light of God's perfection. And then we are told that in the same instant that the sin is confessed the seraph touched his mouth and said, "Your guilt has departed and your sin is blotted out"—and that's the third step. God's love filled Isaiah's heart and he knew that he was forgiven, but only after his confession and his forgiveness was he able to hear God's call: "Whom shall I send, and who will go for us?" And Isaiah said (and in response to God's forgiveness and love there was no other answer), "Here am I; SEND ME!" The fourth step was finished, and the making of a prophet and a leader had begun. Isaiah was now God's child.

And Isaiah goes on to speak God's word to a blind,
resistant people. You remember what follows the call. God
says, "Go forth...do not unstop the ears, do not have the
blind see...." But the very important piece that follows it
(and it's my Orthodox sisters and brothers who have
taught me so much this last year who said, "What's with
you Protestants? You always forget the last part of it!")
basically says: it isn't about hearing and it isn't about
seeing and it isn't about the mind, but turn to God and be
healed. And then it says, "How long, O Lord?"

Then Isaiah set before the people a vision of the new
Jerusalem, but it is God's vision, not Isaiah's vision. Listen
to the words of the 65th chapter:

> Be glad and rejoice forever in what I am creating;
> for I am about to create Jerusalem as a joy.... No
> more shall the sound of weeping be heard in it, or
> the cry of distress. No more shall there be in it an
> infant that lives but a few days, or an old person
> who does not live out a lifetime....They shall build
> houses and inhabit them; they shall plant vineyards
> and eat their fruit. They shall not build and another
> inhabit; they shall not plant and another eat. My
> chosen shall long enjoy the work of their hands.
> ...They shall not labor in vain, or bear children for
> calamity....The wolf and the lamb shall feed
> together....They shall not hurt or destroy on all my
> holy mountain.
>
> Isaiah 65:18–25

Can you imagine how that sounds in Los Angeles, in
the churches today? This is the vision of a world made new.
Isaiah knew from his own life experience the importance of
a vision that sets before us a higher order of love and
justice, of peace and unity. This, my friends, is what is
missing in all the talk about a New World Order. The lack
of a vision is what makes our election rhetoric so disturb-
ing. There is no vision of an America where justice and
compassion would reign in alabaster cities that stretch

from sea to shining sea and where the bountiful resources of a favored land would be thankfully received and gladly shared with the whole of the human family.

It is not that the candidates don't have the right speech writers. It is not about rhetoric. It's about spiritual blindness, and the President is not alone. Our failure as a nation to be captured by God's vision of how it ought to be makes us then captive to how it is. And we can only tinker with the machinery. It is only when we see and understand God's vision for God's people that we can bow the knee and say in a truly confessional way that we have sinned and fallen short of the glory of God. This is what we need to heal this nation.

This is what we want and need in our national leaders. We need leaders who have seen God. We need leaders with Isaiah's vision, who in the light of that understanding look with pain at what is and say, "How can we do this? Infants that live but a few days; old people who live out their lives in poverty; young people captive to addiction begging for treatment and offered jail as the only option; too many who bear children for calamity and labor in vain and build houses for others to inhabit...and violence that begets violence...."

Most serious of all is that we are getting used to it. In the 1990s we're getting used to the idea that 50 percent of black men under the age of thirty will do time, just as in the 1980s we got used to the fact that millions of Americans must live on the street. Perhaps the burning of Los Angeles will wake us up from our lethargy and move us to action. God forbid that we should get used to the burning of our cities. Our moral outrage is muted, our ecumenical voice is weak, and we seem no longer to see the vision nor confess our inadequacies nor respond to God's quick and complete forgiveness for our human weaknesses, and because of it we fail to respond to God's call: "Whom shall I send, and who will go for us?"

Does it matter that we recognize the real state of this nation? Indeed it does, because we are citizens of the United States of America, the reigning power in this world, and our decisions spell life or death for millions. How we see ourselves, how we act, who we choose as leaders matters very much.

So in an election year, perhaps we might ask of those who would choose to be our national leaders if they have seen a vision—not if they have one they can articulate, but if they have seen and internalized God's vision and God's holiness. Ask them, if in their heart of hearts, they know what it means to speak the words HOLY, HOLY, HOLY. Ask them if they know that they are sinners—not in the way the media asks of Bill Clinton or the FBI of Martin Luther King before him, for we don't lead out of our perfection, but out of our comprehension of God's holiness, God's vision, and out of our humility and out of our gratefulness for God's grace and forgiveness. Ask them if they understand that even if Isaiah's vision cannot be reached, that it must be reached for. Ask them if they know that it is God who leads. Ask them if they know they are forgiven. Ask them if, in the flickering candleglow of an evening, they can hear God's call.

And then, as people of faith, we know we have no right to ask these questions, nor to judge the answers unless we have asked them of ourselves, of our church leaders, of our business leaders, of our teachers, of our scientists, of our children. Do we have deep in our souls a vision that is not nation-bound, nor bound by race, nor by our economic status? Do we have a vision that is consonant with Jesus' prayer that we might be one?

It was no accident that it was in the shadow of the cross, in the face of danger and death and despair, that Jesus prayed for unity. Jesus knew that by our very nature it would be difficult for us to see the vision of oneness. It is a vision that even found its way into our national rhetoric. We speak of forming a more perfect union. Yet even today, in the midst of tremendous disillusion, despair, and disunity, we can know that we have no less than the Lord of history praying for us, and calling us to come to the table that is set for all God's people everywhere, in all times and in all places.

Postscript:

Did it matter that we went to Los Angeles, that we were simply present at the time of need? Here are the words of Rev. Cecil Murray, pastor of the First AME Church of Los Angeles:

My dear friend,

Your presence brought more joy than you can possibly imagine. We are revived by your visit, by the gift of your inspiring love, and by your desire to be a part of us.

The dream of community can and must be a reality. This conflagration will not endure. The old foundations are being torn down. The new will rise as a phoenix from the ashes.

Watch!

We love you!

Sincerely,

Cecil L. Murray